PRAISE FOR

Putin's Exiles

"Starobin's hands-on examination of Russia's exile community
is a remarkable story of brave people looking to the future."
Kirkus Reviews

"Paul Starobin's richly reported and shrewdly argued essay
poses a provocative question: could the more than a million
Russians who have left Russia since Putin launched his war
on Ukraine be a factor in the downfall of Putin's imperial
autocracy? Starobin examines the disparate motives of this
new diaspora and, without overstating the case, concludes
that 'the exiles are an actor and possibly an author of the
outcome.'"
BILL KELLER,
former Moscow correspondent
and executive editor of the *New York Times*

"This short volume is a must-read for anyone who cares
about the future of Russia and Ukraine, and the cascading
consequences of Putin's aggression for the wider world.
Starobin has crafted an efficient, highly readable field guide
to the interlocking ambitions, relationships, and origins
of Russia's new exiles, reflecting careful research into both
individual stories and broader context. Those whose lives and
work intersect with *Putin's Exiles* will come back again and
again to mine this book's rich veins of profile and dialogue."
MATTHEW ROJANSKY,
president and CEO of The US Russia Foundation

"Paul Starobin offers a timely snapshot of the mass exodus of Russians seeking to avoid complicity in Russia's war in Ukraine. His narrative is action-packed and artfully contextualized within the arc of Russian and Soviet history, and its fast pacing reflects the speed with which his protagonists left Russia. This book is a must-read for anyone who wants to understand the myriad motivations of exiled Russians and their ardent desires to shape their country's future."

Putin's Exiles
Their Fight for a Better Russia

COLUMBIA GLOBAL REPORTS
NEW YORK

Putin's Exiles
Their Fight for a Better Russia

Paul Starobin

Putin's Exiles
Their Fight for a Better Russia
Copyright © 2024 by Paul Starobin

Published by Columbia Global Reports
91 Claremont Avenue, Suite 515
New York, NY 10027
globalreports.columbia.edu
facebook.com/columbiaglobalreports
@columbiaGR

Library of Congress Cataloging-in-Publication Data

Names: Starobin, Paul, author.
Title: Putin's exiles : their fight for a better Russia / Paul Starobin.
Description: New York, NY : Columbia Global Reports, 2024. | Includes
    bibliographical references.
Identifiers: LCCN 2023038249 (print) | LCCN 2023038250 (ebook) |
    ISBN 9798987053607 (paperback) | ISBN 9798987053614 (ebook)
Subjects: LCSH: Political refugees—Russia (Federation) | Russians—Foreign
    countries—History—21st century. | Russians—Political activity—Foreign
    countries. | Protest movements—Russia (Federation) | Russia (Federation)—
    Politics and government—21st century.
Classification: LCC DK35.5 .S737 2024 (print) | LCC DK35.5 (ebook) |
    DDC 325/.2109470905—dc23/eng/20230925
LC record available at https://lccn.loc.gov/2023038249
LC ebook record available at https://lccn.loc.gov/2023038250

Book design by Strick&Williams
Map design by Jeffrey L. Ward
Author photograph by Nargiza Yuldasheva

Printed in the United States of America

To Nargiza

CONTENTS

"To Fix Russia"

Perhaps you are familiar with the Edvard Munch painting *Evening: Melancholy on the Beach*. A young man sits alone by the sea, a weary chin propped on a dejected hand. The work serves as the jacket illustration for *The Oxford Book of Exile,* a romp through the experiences of peoples made or driven to leave their homelands for one reason or another over the millennia. This is a common depiction of exile, as an unhappy phase in life, marked by isolation and inaction. While I was not sure just what I would find, one reason for embarking on this book was to challenge this received wisdom on the exile experience. To do so, I cast far and wide to speak with individuals who had taken flight from Russia in the Putin era. I met with dozens of such figures in the former Soviet Republics—now burgeoning Russian exile colonies—of Georgia and Armenia. I spoke by Zoom with exiles in France and Germany, in Britain, Switzerland, Cyprus, and America. I was interested, especially, in exiles active in political opposition to Putin's regime but this was not my exclusive concern, as I aimed for a general understanding of the exile experience and mindset.

14   My subjects ranged from the director of a commercial advertising agency to a teenaged Bakunin-spouting anarchist and an
Orthodox priest and his wife, an acclaimed musicologist. Some
had known no Russian leader other than Putin for their entire
lives; others were children of the *glasnost* and *perestroika* time
that preceded the collapse of the Soviet Union in 1991.

The in-person talks, as might be expected, were particularly poignant. Over innumerable cups of tea and coffee and the
occasional cognac, many exiles bared their hearts to me. Tales
of their upended lives sometimes brought forth reddened eyes.
Most of those with whom I spoke had fled Russia after Putin
launched his war in Ukraine in February 2022. Others, pressured by Putin's security services, had left years earlier. In a
suburban Boston mansion, a sunlit corner room repurposed
as a shrine to Alexei Navalny, the imprisoned Russian opposition leader, I nibbled on chocolates from Moscow while meeting
with the North American head of the Navalny team's far-flung
operation.

For all the tears, the picture that emerged was on the whole
one of vibrancy and defiance. Putin's exiles were in retreat but
not defeated. In fact, a rebellion was in formation: an uprising that had at its goal the making of a freer, less warlike
Russia, shorn of its evident social pathologies. "We owe this
to the world—to fix Russia," economist Sergei Guriev, a widely
respected wise man among the exiles, told me from his home in
Paris.

The argument of this book is that the rebellion of Putin's
exiles has the potential to achieve its objective of a better
Russia. The rebellion is not a passing phase. It springs from
deep uncowed conviction and can be expected to endure to the

last days of Putin's life, if he is not removed from office before-
hand. The war in Ukraine has started a new epoch in Russian
history, a new chapter in which the exiles are an actor and possibly an author of the outcome.

An important component of this optimistic claim is the
pronounced generational character of the rebellion. I spoke with
many young exiles who described themselves as in revolt from
cowardly parents who failed to stand up against Russia's slide
back into autocracy and imperial aggression under Putin. These
were frequently bitter and painful clashes: the son who left
home on his father's and mother's refusals to join him in speaking out publicly against the Ukraine invasion, even though his
parents privately were against the war; the daughter who faced
the wrath of her mother for participating in an anti-war street
protest; another daughter whose relations with her mother
fractured when her mom declared her to be an enemy of the
state. Sometimes a grandparent was the issue, as for an exiled
journalist who considered his grandfather a zombie creation of
the Russia state's political propaganda but who hoped to save
his grandmother.

Here, then, was a venerable Russian theme that harkened
to Turgenev and his mid-nineteenth-century novel *Fathers and
Sons* (in the original Russian, *Ottsy i Deti*, which translates as
Fathers and Children). "His day is over; his song has been sung
to extinction," Bazarov, the nihilistic medical student, says of
his young friend's father. "We must clear the ground." In this
framework, Putin, the prime target of today's revolt, could be
thought of as a father figure. Russian society has deep and abiding patriarchal roots, a legacy of its Byzantine Orthodox culture, and in this cultural cosmos, the Tsar-like Putin occupies

16   a mythical status as head of the national household. But he turned seventy-one in 2023. What Putin's rebellious children have going for them is their years. They will outlive the father who has so roiled the Russian domicile. And as the savvy among them understand, the time to start clearing the ground is now. The work of patient preparation can be seen in the anti-Putin movement embodied by Alexei Navalny, twenty-four years younger than Putin and—from his prison cell in Russia—the inspiration for legions of committed young Russians in exile.

     The book's argument might sound like a paradox—one must leave the country to change it? Yet such has been the Russian experience. Whatever one thinks of the Russian Revolution, it was unimaginable without the organizing efforts of figures like Lenin and Trotsky in their long years of exile. Consider Lenin's arc. In 1897, at the age of twenty-six, he was sentenced by the Tsar's court to, in effect, internal exile in Siberia, and three years later, with that time served, he departed for Western Europe. In 1902, he published his galvanizing pamphlet, *What Is to Be Done?* from abroad; the following year he participated in congresses of exiled Russians in Brussels and London. Fourteen years went by before, in the spring of 1917, he departed his one-room apartment in Zurich, passed through Europe on a 2,000-mile journey on a sealed train, and arrived at the Finland Station in the imperial capital of St. Petersburg to take charge of the Bolshevik insurrection and usher in the revolution.

     Then, too, there is the earlier example of Alexander Herzen. In Sergei Guriev's vow "to fix Russia" he sounded much like Herzen, the prototype of the Russian liberal reformer in exile, from a century-and-a-half before. Herzen fled the Russia of Tsar Nicholas 1 because his outspoken convictions, such as the imperative to abolish serfdom, pointed to a life spent in deso-late prison camps. Nicholas I died in 1855, the war he was waging in Crimea headed for failure. His son Alexander II succeeded him at the age of thirty-six, and the young new Tsar ended the war and embarked on systemic reforms, including the liberation of the serfs, aimed at modernizing Russia, just as exiles like Herzen had long called for. Occupied with these internal projects, Russia became less menacing to the world beyond its borders.

The potential for activists abroad to engender dramatic change in their native land is not confined to the Russian case. In China, the seeds for the toppling of the Qing dynasty in 1911 were sowed years earlier with the organization of thousands of Chinese students in Japan into a revolutionary society, the United League, pledged to the "restoration of sovereign power to the Chinese people" and the "establishment of a democratic government and equalization of land rights." Sun Yat-sen, the leader of the revolution who became the first provisional president of the Republic of China, began his frequent visits to the Chinese students in Japan as early as 1905. Just as in the example of the Bolshevik Revolution, change is often slow to come, and then it comes suddenly, all the advantage to those who prepare for the moment.

The logic of the exile as an agent of change, then, is clear enough. In flight from an inhospitable society—and in the Russian experience, exile is traditionally a function of repression—exiles over the ages have used their time to hone their visions of a better order of things. In this sense, the unbid condition of exile can be a creative spur. In the twenty-first century, that is probably true as never before, with the tools of

18   digital communication making for easy connections between
like-minded exiles dispersed across nations and continents.
Putin's exiles connected on chat groups on Telegram, Signal,
and WhatsApp, shared YouTube videos, and formed commit-
tees on which meetings could be held on Zoom. The hive mind
never rested.

The chapters that follow lay out the dynamic and varied character of the anti-Putin, anti-war exile movement. Putin's invasion spurred an epochal flight out of Russia, including leading
cultural, political, media, and business figures. Many exiles
plunged into activities to push back against the Kremlin and
its policies. An information resistance was mounted, expos-
ing Russians back home to the kinds of coverage, as on the war,
that state-controlled media twisted or ignored. Some exiles
actively aided the Ukrainian fight against Russia's armed forces
in hopes of hastening Russia's defeat and Putin's demise. One
even received an award from the Ukrainian armed forces for
his volunteer work in devising a missile-detection system that
enabled the Ukrainian military to shoot down incoming Russian
cruise missiles and attack drones. Dissidents in the Russian
Orthodox Church took sharp aim at Patriarch Kirill, the head
of the Church, for his alliance with the Kremlin and support for
the war. Political activists, led by the Navalny team, cultivated
networks of supporters behind the lines in Russia.

The idea that there could be a better Russia—some exiles
called this a turn to a "True Russia," as a bastion of humanism—
was an animating conviction among many exiles. But it was not
only idealism that prodded Putin's exiles into action. Many
were driven by a consuming hatred of the man himself: Every

day they woke up in hopes of the news that the occupant of
the Kremlin—who openly disparaged the exiles as scum—had
choked to death on his morning porridge. And not least, a sense
of personal guilt, or if not guilt, shame, was a motivating agent
for exiles. The blood of Ukrainians racked their conscience,
even though, as was the case for virtually all Russian exiles, they
opposed Putin's invasion. "Let's imagine that your elder brother
killed somebody," an exile explained to me. "You are not guilty.
But it's still shame for the family." Here was another ripe theme,
the shame of the Russian national family for its manifold
crimes, a wrenching sentiment that summoned the works of
Dostoevsky. In his final novel, *The Brothers Karamazov,* a criminal prosecutor alludes to Russia's "wild, imprudent gallop" as
other nations recoil at "the mad course of our unbridledness."

Perhaps an inner sense of wrong was compounded by the
piercing cry of Ukrainians and others that, as Russia's war
showed, there were no good Russians. Write a book, not about
the hundreds of thousands of Russians who had left their country, but about the millions of Ukrainians forced out of *their*
brutalized homeland, a Ukrainian-American friend pointedly
suggested to me. Fair enough. But the point stands that Putin's
exiles are not in the mold of the static, disconsolate figure
painted by Munch but a potentially history-changing vanguard.

This argument is not immune to rebuttal. It pays to state
the counter-position as vigorously as possible, to bring this
discussion into sharper relief. To start with, the departure of as
many as one million Russians still left behind more than 99 percent of the total population of about 143 million. Even the exit
of hundreds of thousands of draft-eligible men did not appre-
ciably slow the Kremlin's conscription drive. Moreover, many

of those who remained had the means to get out but chose not to. These included artistic types who gave voice to a popular backlash against the exiles. "I'm here because my conscience dictates it," an aging former member of the Russian rock band Aquarius wrote in an open letter from the trenches in Ukraine, addressed to a former bandmate in exile in London. "And neither I, nor those who stand beside me, are fascists, like you say. We are on our own land. We are liberating it from those who seek to destroy everything Russian, our memory, our culture, our church, our thoughts." As this letter suggested, the response to anti-Putin, anti-war exiles could not be attributed simply to the work of Kremlin-directed propagandists. Russian nationalism and imperialism, accompanied by an ingrained opposition to the West, were centuries-old features of a certain Russian outlook and still sustained a distinct idea of what it meant to be Russian. Chauvinists, as adherents to this well-worn perspective might be called, hailed the flight of Russia's leading liberal, pro-Western figures as cause for celebration. "Liberalism in Russia is dead forever, thank God," a pro-Tsar, Orthodox Christian business magnate based in Moscow told the *New York Times* on the one-year anniversary of the Ukraine invasion. "The longer this war lasts, the more Russian society is cleansing itself from liberalism and the Western poison." Russian schoolchildren made candles for the country's troops on the front lines in Ukraine, as their teachers dispensed the lesson that the historical role of Russia's armed forces was to free humanity from "aggressors who seek world domination." Aggressors, in this dichotomy, now meant invaders full of the venom of "NATOzism," a play on Nazism. In stark contrast to the guilt and shame that was a signature feature of Putin's exiles, among at-home Russians only one in ten considered themselves "definitely" responsible for the deaths of Ukrainians, a survey found.

In this environment, Putin's immediate status seemed secure. For all of Russia's problems in the war campaign, he was most vulnerable to challenge, not from anti-war exiles, but from the flank to his right, among those who accused him of ill-preparedness for the war and of flawed strategy and tactics. This peril was illustrated dramatically when, sixteen months into the war, the warlord Yevgeny Prigozhin staged an uprising against Russia's military command and commenced a march on Moscow. Yet in the end Prigozhin stood down, and Putin, even with his prestige damaged by the mutiny, remained in power. At the same time, the anti-Putin exiles were prone to infighting, as is typically the case for exile communities of any national stamp. Jealousies and personal rivalries abounded. The Navalny organization, prideful of its unparalleled reach within Russia, spurned cooperation with like-minded groups in the Russian diaspora. Opposition leaders Mikhail Khodorkovsky and Garry Kasparov had more standing in the West than in Russia. Only a handful of Orthodox priests openly broke with Patriarch Kirill. Amid warnings by the exiles that Putin's war threatened to destroy Russia, the economy, even in the teeth of severe Western sanctions, had not broken down. One reason was that non-Western governments like China, India, Iran, South Africa, and Brazil rejected calls by exiles to isolate Russia by stopping trade with it: Russia still had buyers for its fossil fuel exports and imported consumer goods from China and others. Unfortunately for the exiles, a long-standing view of the West as complicit in imperialism worked against their drive for unified global support for the defeat of Russia in Ukraine. In South

Africa, for example, Putin's Kremlin benefited from the legacy of Moscow's support in Soviet times for militant opponents of the apartheid regime. And even in virulently anti-Putin countries, exiles paid the price of a legacy of distrust of all Russians, as seen in a crackdown by state authorities in Latvia on a media outlet owned and operated by Russians abroad. In such unwelcome terrain, exiles faced the temptation of giving up the struggle against Putin and autocracy and committing to permanent lives elsewhere. Some had done so already.

So goes the counter-argument to the proposition that the exiles can alter the direction of Russia. Still, even with these points taken into account, certain achievements of the exiles appear to be enduring. For one thing, the exiles serve a custodial function in articulating and safekeeping visions of Russia that depart from its autocratic present and past. Autocracies seek not just to suppress dissenting points of view, but even more insidiously, to make it seem as if the only reality, and the only future, is as the state deems. Putin's rule began with a mildly autocratic coloration and has steadily become more repressive, with a decided shift in this direction on the launching of the Ukraine invasion and the Russian government's treatment of dissent as a criminal offense. Because the exiles live outside of this warped milieu, but remain, for a good number, Russian in spirit and identification, they are uniquely able to illuminate better paths for Russia and they have done so. These paths take different shapes. The most common is the route, supported by liberal reformers, that has today's Europe as the destination, Russia taking its place alongside Switzerland, France, Germany et al., as a secular, rule-of-law democracy. Another path, embraced by exiled priests, is an inward journey that sees

Russia's revival in reforms of traditional institutions like the
Russian Orthodox Church, to detach such institutions from
the state and bring them closer to the people. A bridge between
these two streams perhaps can be seen in Navalny, who strad-
dles the Europeanists and the Christian populists. But whether
the agenda for change comes from Westernizers or from inward-
looking types, the essential point is that the exiles are preserv-
ing the counter-possibilities of a better Russia amid the dark
age of Putin's seemingly interminable rule. And the exiles,
given their credibility as demonstrated opponents of the war
and of Putin, can be a powerful force for reconciliation between
Ukraine and a post-Putin, postwar Russia. This will be the
case especially if the exiles can speak to the Ukrainians in the
Ukrainian language, which some exiles are now learning.

Apart from all else, Putin's exiles, in their strivings "to fix
Russia," give the lie to the claims that there are no good Russians.
Even if, in the broadest possible sense, all Russians bear some
guilt for their country's deeds, good works can be redemptive.
Good Russians are nowadays to be found in many places—in
Yerevan, Tbilisi, and the Georgian Black Sea port of Batumi, as
I found in my travels. They can be found among public intel-
lectuals in Paris and London who write manifestos, among
brave exiled journalists who report on Russia's brutal conduct
in Ukraine, among scientists who help Ukraine's military stop
Russia's missiles, and among volunteers who collect garbage on
the streets of their host cities. They can even be found inside of
Russia, as in the political prisoners dispatched to internal exile.
Their commitment to a better Russia is sincere and my hope is
for their success.

Flight
"I Didn't Want to Die"

Early in the morning of February 24, 2022, Alexsei Fisun was awakened by a phone call. He was alone in his Moscow apartment save for Roza, his big fluffy Samoyed. On the other end of the line was Anna, a partner in his commercial advertising agency.

"Do you know what is happening? Russia is bombing Ukraine!" she screamed.

"Oh shit," Fisun replied.

A bell rang in his mind—and in the minds of just about everyone in Russia, with exactly the same dumbfounded reaction. The invasion was a shock. And understandably so, because despite the months-long massing of Russian troops along the border with Ukraine, even Ukraine's president, Volodymyr Zelensky, dismissed the possibility of an all-out invasion—until it happened. The pouring of their country's troops into Ukraine, with a lightning strike aimed at the capital of Kyiv, was nearly impossible for Russians to fathom, even for those in Moscow's political and business circles who thought they

knew Putin's mind. And yet, even though the moment felt both
baffling and overwhelming, a certain instinct, conditioned by
the history of Russia, kicked in. The unexpected is a kind of
normal in the Russian experience. This was a society, after all,
that had experienced, over the past hundred or so years, the
Bolshevik Revolution and the murder of the Tsar followed by
a savage civil war, the terrors of Stalin, and the overthrow of
the Soviet system, with its replacement, a nominally democratic state, regressing into Tsar-like autocracy. The instinct
formed by history—to know in the recesses of one's mind that
at any time could come a thunderbolt that could upend lives—
went much deeper than attitudes toward Putin. Russia's leader
was simply activating a reflex, much as a knee responds when
struck just below the cap.

A bell rang—and then, for many, there was a shudder. What
did the war mean for life in Russia? Instinct suggested repression, a tightening of the screws by the Kremlin, in the first
instance to squelch public dissent and to target known anti-
government voices. For people like Fisun, this prospect was
especially unnerving, because of his volunteer work on behalf
of political opponents of Putin. Was his name already on a list
kept by the security services? In the hours after learning of the
invasion, "I don't think there were rational thoughts," he later
told me, "only emotion. The first emotion was fear for something that might threaten your life." Yet even fear is not mind-
less; it, too, can be guided by instinct. Repression might mean,
many Russians now sensed, not just a lid on dissent, but a "state
of emergency" sealing of national borders. In not-so-distant
Soviet times, for some seventy years, Russians had to live with
severely restricted borders. Only the privileged could leave,

26   with special permission of the state. Open borders—as in the
ability to purchase a plane ticket and visit a relative in Tashkent
or tour Paris—was probably the single most-prized feature of
post-Soviet life.

What to do? Flee. At this moment, Fisun, the creative pro-
ducer at his ad agency, was in the middle of shooting a commercial for one of Russia's largest retailers. At thirty-one years old,
he had worked hard to build up his roster of clients and did not
want to disappoint them. Nevertheless, three days after the invasion, he climbed into his Mazda CX-9 SUV along with Roza and
headed northwest toward the border with Latvia, some seven
hundred kilometers away. Paying no attention to speed lim-
its, he drove at the breakneck pace of 160 kilometers per hour.
Unable to subdue his anxiety—"I was trembling"—he stopped
at a pharmacy to refill a doctor's prescription for Atarax, a sed-
ative. After nearly seven hours, he reached Russia's border with
Latvia. The story he told Russian passport control—a lie—was
that he was leaving Russia to visit his mother in Spain. But it
was a well-chosen fib, for his mother did reside, legally, in Spain,
and Fisun had the documents to prove that. They let him go
through, and the Latvian border authorities gave him no trouble.
Once in Latvia, he found a small, remote hotel with a good internet connection and resumed his work for his clients. Well aware
that many Latvians had scant affections for Russians, even in
the best of times, he fashioned a blue-and-yellow Ukrainian
flag out of some colored paper purchased at a store and made the
flag visible through a window in his Mazda. That step, he felt,
might deflect angry attention from his Russian license plates.

Fisun had plenty of company. In the first three weeks after
the invasion, by mid-March, some 300,000 Russians had left the

country, and by the end of August, probably another 100,000
had departed. At that point, the exodus subsided. Even though
many Western countries, including in Europe, had stopped
accepting direct flights out of Russian airports, Russia had
not, as so many feared at first, sealed its borders. Fisun felt safe
enough to return to his apartment in Moscow. In September,
though, came a fresh jolt: the Kremlin's announcement of a
mass mobilization of recruits for a floundering war in which
tens of thousands of Russian boys already had died. This news
precipitated a second collective dash out of the country, also
numbering in the hundreds of thousands.

Fisun was part of that wave, too. At six feet, three inches tall,
a trim, well-muscled 194 pounds, he was in top physical condition. He was also a lieutenant in the reserve military corps,
his officer status won by his completion of a military training
program as a college student at Moscow State University. He
knew how to fire a gun; he had even spent a month living at an
army base. "I would be a good soldier"—a prized get for combat in Ukraine, he told me. Only there was no way he was going.
"I didn't want to die, first of all," he explained. "Second, I didn't
want to kill." And besides, "our government, it's like a Mafia. I
didn't want to have anything in common with them. Especially
after they started the war."

He determined to head immediately to Yerevan, capital
of Armenia, to which there were direct flights from Moscow.
Russians could enter freely without a visa. He bought a round-
trip ticket, to make it look as if he planned to come back to
Moscow. On arriving at the airport, he found the departure
hall packed with young men sharing the same perilous predic-
ament: "They were all frightened as shit. I looked at them and

28 remembered myself as I was fleeing Russia for the first time. This time, I realized I had no fear. It was okay: just one shitty problem that my government gave me to solve." There was nothing in the official Russian database that revealed his prime 1-A draft status. Hours later, he was safe at a college friend's apartment in Yerevan. His buddy had bought extra mattresses, in anticipation of a tide of incomers.

The one million or so Russians who left the country in the twelve months after the invasion represented an extraordinary number. Early in the Putin period, after he took the reins from Boris Yeltsin, post-Soviet Russia's first president, a trickle of exiles had begun with oligarchs who had fallen out of his favor. Various liberal intellectual types, independent journalists, and disenchanted political and business figures had followed the oligarchs in small numbers. But nothing like this mass flight had occurred in the twenty-three years of his rule. Not since the breakup of the Soviet Union in 1991 had Russia experienced a sudden, large outflow of its populace. The Putin-era dash for the borders reminded, too, of the departure of perhaps as many as two million "white" Russians, after the Bolsheviks came to power in the 1917 Revolution.

To run away from a society at war, from the daunting prospect of military service, is a familiar type of exile. In the nineteenth century, young German men poured into America to escape conscription; in the early twentieth century, it was the Japanese, bound for Peru and Brazil; and decades later, tens of thousands of American boys headed north to Canada to evade the Vietnam draft. But in sheer numbers, over such a short span of time, the exit of the Russians after the invasion probably has no historical parallel. To note this is to underscore the

political element of this flight, even for those in the grip of a
frantic desire to avoid the line of fire. Wartime does not always
spur large numbers of a country's citizens to head for the border. Nothing like this mass exile occurred in any of the nations
involved in World War II. The Russians who left their country
after the invasion were not physical cowards—surely not in any
appreciable numbers. Their homeland was not under attack,
as when Hitler invaded in 1941 and Napoleon in 1812. They
were fleeing a war that made no sense to them. In this mindset, they were kindred spirits with the Americans who sought
sanctuary in Canada to stay out of the jungles of Vietnam.
"It takes a strange mentality to tolerate a war . . . like this," a
twenty-four-year-old who headed to Montreal on receiving
orders to join the US Marines in Vietnam reflected in *The New
Exiles,* a book published in the midst of that war.

Putin's exiles headed mostly for easy-to-reach and fairly
low-cost former Soviet Republics like Armenia and Georgia in
the South Caucasus and Kazakhstan, Uzbekistan, and Kyrgyzstan
in Central Asia. There they clustered in cities in which apartments might be available: Yerevan, as for Fisun, a popular choice;
and Tbilisi, Batumi, Almaty, Tashkent, and Bishkek, too. In
usual times, Batumi, a resort town on the pebbled shores of the
Black Sea in Georgia, hosted large numbers of Russians only in
the summer months. On a trip in December, ten months into the
war, I found the streets and shops crowded with recent Russian
arrivals bundled in winter clothing—"too many" Russians, a
local Georgian complained to me. He said the Russians, flush
with cash, were jacking up rents for apartments to levels beyond
the reach of most of his comparatively poor countrymen. That
was a gripe that now followed Russian migrants everywhere

30   they landed in the former Soviet Union. In Tbilisi, the capital of Georgia, the situation was so bad that university students were having trouble finding housing, I was told.

Aware that their presence could provoke local resentments, some exiles launched projects to establish goodwill in the communities to which they flocked. In garbage-strewn Yerevan, thirty-year-old Dana Vergilyush organized a crew of fellow migrants to go on weekend excursions, equipped with gloves and garbage bags, to clean up targeted sites. Before arriving in Armenia, she had done the same volunteer work in her home city of Rostov-on-Don in southwestern Russia. Some Armenians in Yerevan, she told me, bridled at what they saw as an implicit criticism of the ability of the local population to dispose of their garbage. But the mayor had embraced the initiative and she had become a regular guest on Yerevan's radio and television stations. A governmental official with responsibility for environmental matters even had asked her to make a public-service video highlighting her group's cleanup work. Next, she aimed to help municipal authorities with the arduous task of getting the large number of stray dogs roaming traffic-congested city streets into safe, clean shelters.

Many thousands of Russians headed beyond the territories of the former USSR. Serbia, a traditional Orthodox Christian friend of Russia, was a receptive location. Turkey, a favorite vacation spot for Russians, its airports still open to them, also beckoned. In Antalya, on Turkey's Mediterranean coast, Russians mixed in hotels and bars with war refugees from Ukraine, some wearing national flag armbands. Maybe alcohol was involved, but on occasion, Russians and Ukrainians were seen dancing with each other. Some six thousand miles away in

Bali, they awkwardly met as neighbors in apartment complexes and as workers at jobsites. "I'm sorry, we're from Moscow," a Russian woman explained to a Ukrainian who had mistaken the woman and her colleagues for Ukrainians. For wealthy Russians there was Dubai, with direct flights out of Moscow departing daily.

It soon became difficult for Russian passport holders, even with means, to obtain visas to the European Union amid a rising tide of anti-Russian sentiment. In the Netherlands, a Russian supermarket was vandalized with a brick thrown through the window, and the Haarlam Philharmonic, declaring it "would be inappropriate to celebrate Russian music," canceled a performance of works by Tchaikovsky and Stravinsky. In the United Kingdom, the All England Club banned Russians from the Wimbledon tennis tournament. Some Russians tried to enter the United States through its southern border, as asylum seekers. But at the border they were shunted into detention centers and experienced the miseries, such as inadequate medical care, routinely visited upon migrants seeking admission to America through the chaotic asylum process. "I came to realize that I had left Russia for a place that was just like Russia," an indignant husband, separated from his wife, handcuffed, and knocked to the cement floor by a guard during a transfer of detainees, told the *New York Times*.

The tales of flight could astound. Fisun's sprint to Latvia paled beside the journey made by a pair of Russian men, in flight from military enlistment officers, of hundreds of miles across the Bering Sea in a small fishing craft. Waves threatened to capsize their vessel, but they made safe landing at St. Lawrence Island, a part of Alaska. Then there was a college sophomore's improbable trek out of Kaliningrad, the Russian exclave wedged between Poland and Lithuania on the Baltic seacoast. Faced with expulsion, or worse, for spray-painting "Putin = War" on a wall, the eighteen-year-old bespectacled student, with little more than a blanket and a few liters of water, headed for the border with Poland, twenty miles away. He quickly got lost in the grass-lands and marshes. After three nights, famished to the point of delirium, he found the boundary and crawled under barbed wire to reach Polish territory—only to be taken into custody by authorities and questioned on suspicion of being a Russian spy. Eventually he was released and made it to Paris.

Not everyone was on their own. Some people made it out of Russia with the assistance of secretive anti-war organizations like In Transit, an "underground railroad" set up by a trio of women in St. Petersburg, that provided safe houses, money, and even motor vehicles to escapees. Such efforts showed an age-old Russian talent for outfoxing repressive government. But no matter where the exiles landed, no one, at least no one with a smartphone and an internet connection, was truly isolated. This surely was the best-connected diaspora in human history. Day and night, wherever Wi-Fi was available, these waifs kept in touch by text messages, including with family and friends still back in Russia. With the US-owned WhatsApp platform under threat of being blocked in Russia by the Kremlin, the Telegram channel surged in popularity. Its owner, the multi-billionaire Pavel Durov, was himself a Russian exile who had collided with the Kremlin. He supposedly spent much of his time in Dubai. I hoped to speak with him, but a Russian source in France told me that was probably a fruitless chase: "He is a free electron, as we say in French. He is always everywhere and nowhere."

Putin professed good riddance to deserters of the moth-
erland, as he portrayed those who fled after the invasion. "The
collective West is trying to divide our society," to "use its
fifth column in an attempt to achieve this goal," he declared
three weeks into the war. "But any nation," he continued, "and
even more so the Russian people, will always be able to dis-
tinguish true patriots from scum and traitors and will simply spit them out like an insect in their mouth, spit them onto
the pavement. I am convinced that such a natural and neces-
sary self-purification of society will only strengthen our country, our solidarity, cohesion, and readiness to respond to any
challenges."

Among the so-designated "scum and traitors" who took
flight in the months after the war started was a longtime member of Putin's personal security service. "Our president has
become a war criminal," he said from his place in hiding with his
family. Then there were leading Russian entertainers like iconic
pop singer Alla Pugacheva and her husband, comedian Maxim
Galkin. Russian boys were going to their graves in Ukraine for
"illusory goals," Pugacheva wrote to her several million followers on Instagram. Gone, too, were acclaimed literary figures like
the short-story writer Maxim Osipov. "We hate war, hate the
one who unleashed it, but we also weren't planning to abandon
our homeland," he wrote on boarding a plane for Frankfurt and
feeling, at that very moment, "cold, ashamed, relieved." More
meaningfully to Russia's immediate circumstances, Moscow
and St. Petersburg, the country's two most important metrop-
olises, lost large numbers of highly educated information technology (IT) workers. Such people were fairly confident they
could perform their jobs remotely, from outside of Russia. In

34 all, some 10 percent of the country's information technology workers left Russia in 2022, according to the government's Communications Ministry.

The exodus had a profound impact on the Russia psyche. It split families between the departed and the stayed behind, and created, in this way, a divided nation. In the usual Russian fashion, the exiles tried to cope with their trauma through humor. There were "five stages of coming to terms with the invasion," one joke went: "denial, anger, making deals, depression, Kazakhstan." Underneath the humor, the exiles struggled to process their raw feelings and they asked themselves the most practical of questions: For how long would their Russian bank cards still work? For how long would their host countries permit them to stay? Could residency papers be obtained?

As exiles everywhere are prone to do, they discovered reasons to quarrel. Some "first-wave" Russians looked down on their "second-wave" compatriots for leaving only after Putin announced his mobilization drive. The second-wave contingent consisted largely of provincial rubes—the Russian equivalent of American "rednecks"—a first-wave exile informed me. It was probably true that the first wave contained a higher proportion of well-educated, knowledge-class types from big cities like Moscow and St. Petersburg than did the second wave. And maybe the first-wave group possessed a greater degree of political consciousness—they didn't need a mobilization order to apprehend the threat of Putin. Still, this seemed like an instance of the narcissism of small differences. In their new "homes," no matter when or why they left Russia, all of the exiles were uniformly at risk of being tarred as pariahs. They faced the same challenges of daily life. Their lot was the same.

For how long would they stay out of Russia? For some of those who left, the answer was forever. Determined to be as far from Russia as geographically possible, tens of thousands of middle- and upper-income émigrés, among them large numbers of pregnant women and their husbands, resettled in the Argentine capital of Buenos Aires. "My daughter will be born here, and she will be Argentine," a thirty-one-year-old married woman from Moscow declared. "It's a ticket for the whole family to be safe from the government in Russia." But many others who had fled hoped to return. A slogan cropped up in the diaspora: PPZ. The acronym was a play on VVP, the initials of Vladimir Vladimirovich Putin. For how long to keep away from Russia? *Poka Putin Zhiv*, "While Putin Lives," was the response.

Guilt
"We Killed So Many People"

"Are we guilty?" The question was put to me, unprompted, by the Russian writer Anna Starobinets. We were having an evening drink at a bookstore in Tbilisi owned by a friend of hers. Set before her was a flask of hot grog filled with slices of pears; I was sipping from a glass of Armenian cognac. (The similarity of our unusual family names had us wondering whether we might be relatives, but that seemed unlikely.) From her home in Moscow before the war, Starobinets was a critical and commercial success as a writer, best known for her fictional tales for young readers. The Russian film industry was committed to bringing her stories to cinematic life. She was bound for a wildlife expedition in Sri Lanka to gather material for her next book project. All this, and she was still in her early forties. But now, for fleeing Russia and taking a stand "against the Russian aggression and Putin's regime," as she put it, she expected any day to be branded a "foreign agent" by the Kremlin. And "when that happens, I will have no right to sell books to kids in Russia." Meanwhile, her Georgian landlord, eager to get her and her young son to leave

their apartment to re-lease the place for more money, came
and went as he pleased. If she didn't like it, he informed her,
she could go back to Russia. A further reminder of her dimin-
ished status came on her daily dog walks. "No Russian is welcome, good or bad," someone had scrawled in bold black letters
on the front of a neighborhood building. "Fuck Russia" graffiti
could be seen everywhere in Tbilisi. Back in Moscow, her father
sympathized with her plight. But her mother decidedly did not:
An enthusiastic backer of Russia's war in Ukraine, she considered her daughter an "enemy of the state." The two were no longer on speaking terms.

Her blue eyes fixed on me, I tried to dodge Starobinets's
question with one of my own: You are asking me to be your
judge? But she persisted, saying she only wanted my opinion.

Guilt? There was a lot to unpack. By "we," I took her to
mean Russians collectively. As for what they might be guilty of,
first, of course, was Russia's invasion of Ukraine. At the time
of our get-together, ten months into the war, at least 100,000
Ukrainian soldiers had been killed or injured. Russian soldiers
were credibly accused of rape and torture of Ukrainian civilians.
The Kremlin's own stated strategy was to destroy the enemy's
physical infrastructure to exact submission from a freezing and
starving populace. Russian bombs had struck orphanages, kin-
dergartens, and maternity hospitals. Ukrainian children were
being deported to holding camps in Russia for the purpose
of reeducating the children, as old as seventeen years, in the
Russian government's approved version of Russian culture and
history, with some camps providing military training as well.
A kind of war machine, its gears engaging the Russian bureau-
cracy, suggested a seepage of guilt into the wider society. Were

38 the teachers at these reeducation camps guilty? The cooks that prepared the children's breakfasts?

But I don't think Starobinets had only the war in mind. As seen by many exiles, the war was an outgrowth of Putin's authoritarian and insufficiently challenged rule. His control orientation began mildly on taking power in 2000, but gradually the pressures were ratcheted up: oligarchs jailed, media critics made to toe the line, opposition political parties at first barely tolerated, then not at all. Putin, eight years into his tenure, stepped back from the presidency, but he remained in government and returned as president four years later, seemingly as a Tsar for life. State violence became more overt, as with the near-fatal poisoning of Navalny in 2020. Many Russians took to the streets to protest crackdowns on their liberties. Most, though, settled for the implicit bargain held out by the Kremlin: Stay out of politics, and your private life is your own.

Perhaps it was "the bargain," as Russians commonly called this transaction, that weighed on Starobinets. Many Russians had come to regret their elevation of personal ambitions, their desire for security for themselves and their families, above a civic obligation to take a stand against increasingly brutish governance. People all over the world routinely made this sort of choice, of course, but now, in Russia, the price for this bargain had been starkly revealed. I answered her that probably yes, all Russians were guilty, though in widely varying degrees. She nodded; surely, I was just echoing her own settled thoughts.

Some exiles labored to divorce themselves from Putin and his deeds—to couch his "personal madness," as one person in Yerevan said to me, as entirely outside of Russian culture and experience. But this was unusual. The striking thing, as in this instance with Starobinets, was how readily the matter of guilt came to the fore in my conversations with Russian exiles. A confessional impulse seemed at work. And this was true especially for the most accomplished, the most distinguished, of the exiles. No one in the exile community had greater stature than the celebrated economist Sergei Guriev. He left Russia in 2013 on fear of imprisonment by Putin's security services for his support for political opponents of the Kremlin, and he was now a professor at Sciences Po in Paris. His disposition on the whole was a sunny and practical one: His name recurs throughout this book because he was a leader in organizing initiatives undertaken by exiles to counter Russia's war in Ukraine and Putin's autocratic rule generally. Exiles in political, financial, and media circles often sought his advice. He was just fifty years old when the war began, and admirers pictured him as a prime minister, or some such lofty station, in a post-Putin Russian government. Yet when he first talked to me on Zoom, from his home in Paris, he had a weight to get off his chest: "It is very personal, actually. I feel responsible for not standing up to Putin. That is painful." A month later, in our second Zoom conversation, he again reprimanded himself: "I am one of those people who screwed up." This seemed like a harsh judgment. His sins did not seem to go beyond serving on the board of a state-controlled bank and advising Putin's Kremlin to undertake sensible reforms like lessening the Russian economy's dependence on fossil fuels. Still, these associations marked him, in his estimation, as a Putin collaborator.

Over dinner in Tbilisi, a well-educated, politically sophisticated Georgian, attuned to sentiments in the Russian community in his hometown, said he distrusted Russian expressions

40   of guilt. This felt like empty rhetoric, a ritual nod to local sensibilities now that Russians were guests in the houses of others, he told me. I could see his point, but still, I thought he was wrong. Guilt and its close cousin, shame, mostly struck me as heartfelt. To see images of slaughtered Ukrainians was unbearable, a Russian exile in London weepingly told me: "We killed so many people." It seemed to me, too, that guilt and shame could be a key to understanding the exiles in deed—to grasping their manifold efforts to counter the Kremlin from abroad even at the risk of becoming targets of Putin's roaming security services or of facing imprisonment or a bar on employment on return to Russia. In fact, I came to think it was not possible to assess the prospects of the exile community without a purchase on these haunting sentiments.

Sergei Guriev was a case in point: He now spoke to me of his "duty" to make up for his personal failings, as if this was a matter of honor. But my realization of the power of guilt struck me most sharply in a lengthy conversation with a young, Russian-trained physician. I met Nastya (short for Anastasia) in Yerevan, at the local offices of a nonprofit, The Ark, run by Russian exiles. The group dispensed assistance to members of the swollen Russian diaspora as they tried to adjust to their suddenly changed circumstances. The Ark's director in Yerevan had sent out a general invitation for exiles to join me for an open-ended discussion of their thoughts and experiences, and more than a dozen showed up for the occasion. On the walls were framed watercolor paintings of Russian anti-war protests. Psychotherapy was among the services offered by The Ark, and as the meeting stretched for hours, I felt at times to be in a group-therapy session, improbably cast as the therapist. Or maybe this was more like a mutual-support exercise: Everyone applauded when one participant, Irina, said just that day she had received her permit to stay in Armenia as a permanent resident. Nastya was quiet throughout, but at the end of the event, she introduced herself to me, and on an impulse, I invited her to dinner.

We reconvened at a restaurant a few minutes' walk from Yerevan's Republic Square. At that point I knew only her first name, as with the rest of those I had met with at The Ark. Many exiles preferred to keep it that way to stay out of the ill graces of Russian authorities and perhaps future employers back in Russia. Nastya, though, wrote her full name for me on my notepad—"I am comfortable telling my surname"—and allowed me to take her picture, her wisps of light blonde hair straying across a reddened, anxious face. Thirty-one years old, she described herself as "a simple village girl" from Karelia, a region of northwest Russia bordering Finland. And then she launched a barrage of verbiage aimed squarely at herself: "I feel guilty of being childish, of being illiterate, of being indifferent to politics. I believed I was too stupid to know about politics, as my mother told me." She began to wise up in her years at the medical institute in St. Petersburg, but even so, she scrupulously refrained from any open display of criticism of Putin. "I was afraid to take part in actions in Russia," she related to me. "I was afraid to be beaten. And as a medical student I would have been expelled. At that time, I would have preferred to be shot in the head than lose my medical diploma."

But the war, its horror, broke her embrace of "the bargain." She left Russia with her husband, an IT worker who kept a distance from politics. In Yerevan, she took part in a public antiwar

42   protest, a coming-out for her. Her mother saw a photograph of
      her at the protest, published in the Russian press, and lost it.
      Over the phone, she screamed at Nastya, accusing her daughter
      of being a paid propaganda tool of the anti-Russian camp. The
      next day, though, she called Nastya back and said she accepted
      her motives as sincere.

      Nastya told me that, in present circumstances, she could not
      imagine returning to Russia. Her dream was to visit Ukraine, to
      help rebuild the country after the war, should Russians like her
      be allowed into the country. She realized that her wish might
      never be fulfilled, but nonetheless she was taking classes to
      learn the Ukrainian language. On our parting after the dinner,
      she told me that she had felt nervous about coming to meet me
      but now felt relieved for having spoken her mind so thoroughly.
      I was left with the impression of a painfully earnest young per-
      son whose deep sense of guilt was, not a source of paralysis, but
      a catalyst for a replotted life's journey of uncertain destination.
      She seemed as if she had had an epiphany.

      Might the war have given life to such a type as the "woke
      Russian," with no irony intended in the use of that term? There
      were many tropes in Russian culture that evoked the insignifi-
      cant, weak-willed Russian, as in the protagonist in Turgenev's
      Diary of a Superfluous Man, who observed that the world regarded
      him "like an unexpected and uninvited guest." In response, he
      sunk into torpor. But this habit of passivity, as Russian history
      also showed, could be broken, even if it took a crisis like a war to
      spur engagement. In the case of the Ukraine invasion, genera-
      tional friction also supplied a prod: The bond between mother
      and daughter can be the closest of any familial tie, but as for

Nastya and also for Anna Starobinets, the war was a profound source of discord in that relationship. They were in painful exile not just from their native country but from the person who brought them into the world.

Although Nastya presented an especially anguished case of the guilt felt by exiles, her determination to learn the Ukrainian language was not particularly unusual among her peers. This was not an easy feat for a Russian speaker. Even though the thirty-three-letter Ukrainian alphabet was nearly identical to the Russian alphabet—both were Slavic languages—there were differences in pronunciation, verb and noun endings, and various grammatical features. Many Ukrainians had learned Russian, but the reverse was much less likely to be true. In Yerevan, language classes were offered by the Ukrainian Forum, a tiny nonprofit that assisted Ukrainian refugees with resettlement in Armenia. On a visit to her modest offices, the director, Olena Shevchuk, a native of the Ukrainian port city of Odesa, told me that she had three groups of pupils studying Ukrainian, mostly made up of Russian exiles. And Nastya's dream, the director added, was common among the Russians in Yerevan: "Many say they want to go to Ukraine after the war, to restore it."

To feel guilty can activate the desire to do penance and it seemed like that was what I was glimpsing in exiles like Nastya. Learning the official language of the nation being obliterated by Putin was a step, at least, on the road to amends. So, too, were personal apologies to Ukrainians. At Olena Shevchuk's Ukrainian Forum, I met with a Ukrainian mother and daughter whose village home had been destroyed by Russian forces. The daughter told me that Russians in Yerevan often expressed

44   to her their sorrow they didn't do more to change the Putin gov-
     ernment. They should feel guilty, she told me, but still, "I see
     most of them are good people and want to help Ukraine."

     Sergiy Petrenko, a Ukrainian who lived in Odesa, was the
     former head of Ukrainian operations for Yandex, the Moscow-
     based tech company. When the war began, he volunteered for
     the Red Cross in Odesa and devoted his time to humanitarian
     relief. "Well, in general, I myself am ready to accept any help in
     rebuilding our country," he told me in an exchange on Telegram.
     But he predicted that some Russians, genuinely beset with guilt
     but nonetheless possessed of an ingrained overlord mental-
     ity, would not be able to resist the impulse to demand recog-
     nition of their "authority" from the Ukrainians these "helpers"
     had come to assist. And so, "anyone who has Russian roots—
     even someone who has participated in active protests" against
     the war—"must understand that he will have no opportunity
     to advise, and even the most sincere opinion will be met with
     prejudice" by Ukrainians, Petrenko told me.

     In sounding this advance note of warning, Petrenko was not
     wrong to flag the imperial attitude as a standard feature of the
     Russian mindset. This bearing was so thoroughly implanted,
     starting with childhood history teachings, that many Russians
     were hardly aware they exhibited it. Russians were not unique in
     this regard. Who in twenty-first-century America, apart from
     a small faction on the Left, considered America to be an impe-
     rial nation, notwithstanding a centuries-long pattern of swal-
     lowing territories, like Texas and California, held by a foreign
     power, and of establishing overseas military bases? In the case
     of Russia, a similar sort of Manifest Destiny reigned as an ide-
     ology for a people that had swept eastward across a continent to

stop only at their side of the Pacific. In Putin's telling, Ukraine, the home of the first Rus, eternally belonged to Russia, and many Russians believed that. In Tsarist times, after all, Ukraine was officially known as "Little Russia."

Habits of thought were difficult to overcome. Still, guilt and shame were of proven utility as tools for even the most aggressive of societies to overcome their destructive ways. The stellar example in modern times was Germany after World War II. It was not just a matter of paying reparations to Holocaust survivors. Germans engaged in a generations-long process of coming to terms with their murderous deeds. There was even one of those impossibly long German words for this regimen: *vergangenheitsaufarbeitung*—"working off the past" in rough translation. "Working off Germany's criminal past was not an academic exercise; it was too intimate for that," Susan Neiman noted in her 2019 book, *Learning from the Germans*. "It meant confronting parents and teachers and calling their authority rotten." And this effort, she noted, had made postwar Germany "far more trusted, even occasionally admired, by the rest of the world," to the point that "many other nations ask Germany to play a more powerful role in world affairs, a request that would have seemed incredible just thirty years earlier."

Of course, the Germans worked off the past only after the Nazis were routed in World War II, with the military occupation of West Germany by the US, Britain, and France stretching for ten years after the war's end. The Allied authorities even decreed, by law, that "the Prussian State, which from early days has been a bearer of militarism and reaction in Germany, has ceased to exist." Among all the ways for the war in Ukraine to conclude, a march on Moscow followed by Western occupation

46 of Russia and a mandated abolition of autocracy seemed an
extremely distant possibility. Moreover, Russians, like many
peoples, had long struggled to come to terms with their soci-
etal crimes. It wasn't until Stalin died, in 1953, that acknowl-
edgment of his routine practice of execution, torture, and
imprisonment was made, and even then, the denunciation, by
Nikita Khrushchev, came in a closed session of the Communist
Party. In the late 1980s, in the spirit of openness—*glasnost*—
inspired by the last Soviet leader, Mikhail Gorbachev, the dis-
sident Andrei Sakharov and his activist wife, Yelena Bonner,
founded Memorial, a nonprofit dedicated to unearthing the
horrors of the Gulag. Lists of victims were compiled, personal
testimony was taken, archives intended to be permanent were
created. But Putin's officials deemed this the work of "foreign
agents" aimed at creating "a false image of the USSR as a terrorist state." In 2021, the Russian government shuttered Memorial.

Even so, the war in Ukraine, amid Putin's insistence that
Russia was merely fulfilling a national calling, no matter the
cost in blood, now jarred some who had fled Russia to reflect
on an imperial past that they never before felt reason to mull. In
Tbilisi, I had tea with Andrey, a smartly dressed recent arrival
from Moscow, a manager of fashion retail shops, several years
shy of forty. He had left Russia to escape conscription and
hoped to bring his wife and their three young daughters, still in
Moscow, to Germany. Far from holding radical political views, he
leaned conservative in his opinions and thought wistfully of the
early Putin years as a needed corrective to the chaotic Yeltsin
period of the 1990s, when Russia lurched from one financial crisis to another. Russia seemed stable then, he thought, a good
environment for starting a career and raising a family. We were

seated in a hotel stocked with Russian guests, yet while many members of the staff knew Russian, the official policy of the establishment was to refrain from use of the "oppressor's" language. Almost none of the Russians spoke Georgian, an ancient Kartvelian language indigenous to the South Caucasus, so they stumbled along as best they could in English.

This was humbling for Russians like Andrey. In the typical Russian mind, Georgia was little more than a place for bracing mountain excursions and tasty food and wine. Yet confronted with intense anti-Russian sentiments along with exuberant partisanship for the Ukrainian cause, Andrey was responding not with defensiveness but a sincere effort at understanding the Georgian perspective. He grasped that Georgians felt bruised by the small losing war they fought with Russian invaders in 2008, as a result of which Russian troops continued to occupy parts of Georgian territory. But he had come to realize, aided by excursions he made outside of Tbilisi to historical sites, that this fairly recent wound was part of a primal trauma at the heart of Georgia's relationship with its giant neighbor to the north.

The story, as Andrey had come to see, was typical of imperial entanglements that create lasting resentments. Imperial Russia arrived in the tiny Kingdom of Georgia late in the eighteenth century with guarantees to protect Georgians from the encroachments of the Ottoman and Persian empires. But Russia swiftly betrayed these assurances, as Georgia, however tempting to the Tsar, was still seen, as a historian later noted, as "an 'expendable' territory beyond the desired Imperial frontier." Russia, in time, formally annexed Georgia and turned Tiflis, as Tbilisi was then called, into a colonial base for further imperial expansion in the Caucasus. The "Russification" of Georgia sped

48 along with Georgian youth journeying to the imperial capital in St. Petersburg to learn the poetry of Pushkin. Georgia enjoyed a brief independence after the Bolsheviks seized power in 1917, but its republic was snuffed out by an invasion of the Red Army and Georgia was made part of the USSR. It wasn't until 1991 that Georgia regained independence.

"Fuck Russia," then, had a long history behind it. Andrei Loshak, a seasoned Russian journalist who specialized in film documentaries, told me that he had left Russia for Tbilisi six years before the war in Ukraine started and felt "very comfortable" with the anti-Russia graffiti around town. Russians, he said, had earned their guilt—"we are a deeply troubled society, as a disease not cured"—and it was better to see those scrawls than the "Z" symbol on display in Russia to show support for Putin's war. Still, as Loshak recognized, an awakened consciousness among exiles, an acceptance of Russian complicity in a long sequence of events that stretched to the invasion of Ukraine, was of little consequence without an impact on hearts and minds inside Russia. Truth-telling journalism, he was convinced, could make a difference, and he was joined in this belief by colleagues who also had taken flight from Russia and now sought to regroup. From their precarious sanctuaries, they gathered a challenge to the state-controlled media machine in Russia that worked without rest to mold popular attitudes to the Kremlin's thinking.

The Information Resistance
"I Think I Can Save My Grandmother"

So far as the Kremlin was concerned, the war in Ukraine was a "special military operation." To call the "operation" an actual war was made a crime, punishable by time in prison. A Russian parliamentarian suggested that journalists who "spread panic" with false news should consider themselves lucky for facing the prospect of a mere fifteen-year sentence. In World War II, he noted, such types were "shot on the spot." At the same time, state-controlled media inundated the public with the official line on what Russia sought to accomplish: the prevention of a genocide perpetrated by the illegitimate Ukrainian regime against innocent ethnic Russians in Ukraine. It was an outlandish claim that nonetheless won lurid repetition as state media scaled back their usual entertainment offerings in favor of more intensive coverage of the confrontation over Ukraine. In a nationally televised ceremony at the Kremlin, Putin gave an award to one of the state's most faithful media personages, Margarita Simonyan, editor in chief of the RT television network. "Thank you for wresting our people out of the bloody

50   mouths of these man-eaters, despite the pain and the blood,"
Simonyan said to her president in a reference to Ukrainian
"aggressors." "And we will help you whack these man-eaters as
much as you demand it from us," she pledged.

In these circumstances, nearly all of the independent-
minded journalists still left in Russia took the one sensible
route available to them: out of the country. "No to war," a defi-
ant Natalya Sindeyeva, the CEO of TV Rain, Russia's last independent television station, declared as the lights went out on its
final broadcast from Moscow, one week into the war. And then,
in sardonic homage to the occasion, the channel aired a few bars
from *Swan Lake*, the Tchaikovsky ballet that state television
endlessly played back in 1991 as geriatric hardliners, behind the
scenes, haplessly tried to keep the USSR from collapsing.

Most of the TV Rain crew regrouped in Riga, joining a cadre
of exiled Russian journalists already based in the Latvian capital, and some of the channel's staff headed for Tbilisi and
set up a satellite bureau there. Twelve years after its launch
in Moscow—as an independent outlet, but not one set up in
explicit opposition to Putin's rule—TV Rain was now all in as
part of what could be called the "information resistance" waged
by Russian news organizations in exile. The goal was to counter
the pro-war, pro-Putin line of state-controlled media in Russia,
and in doing so persuade the public to reject the Kremlin's
approved narrative. It was an ambitious mission, and like any
guerrilla operation mounted from afar against a more power-
fully equipped force, it certainly would not be easy. TV Rain's
saga offers a window into the obstacles faced by "the resistance"
as these insurgents sought to reconstitute their operations in

foreign lands, the impediments arising even in places that were deeply hostile to the Kremlin.

In one sense there was nothing new here. For Russians living in Russia to be fed a diet of unauthorized news and sharp opinion about their country's deeds by compatriots in exile—this was an old story. In the 1850s, in the wake of a failed war fought by Tsarist Russia against Britain, France, and the Ottoman Empire, a Russian émigré in London, Alexander Herzen, launched the publication of a weekly newspaper, *The Bell* (*Kolokol* in Russian). Herzen, an impassioned liberal opponent of autocracy, was a brilliant polemicist—an artful practitioner of "revolutionary journalism" as an admirer later said. But what made *The Bell* a sensation inside of Russia—must reading in the highest reaches of the state, supposedly even by the Tsar—was its access through secret channels in Russia to compelling documentary evidence of corruption and injustices in the Tsar's kingdom. In classic muckraking fashion, *The Bell* exposed Russia's rot.

Herzen had to content himself with print. A century-and-a-half later, in the age of the internet, Russian exiles had many ways to spread their subversive message to the people of their native land. There was social media, of course, but above all other digital platforms, there was Google's YouTube. As puzzling as it seemed to the exiled journalists, the Kremlin had not yet blocked YouTube. No one was quite sure why. The most common explanation was that most Russians did not go to YouTube to obtain oppositionist political fare from the likes of TV Rain. Parents relied on YouTube for their entertainment; their children for cherished cartoons. For the government to shut down

52   YouTube—this would rankle users all over Russia and create an unwelcome political headache for the Kremlin. That was what exiled journalists surmised, anyway.

The exiles also had one over Herzen and *The Bell* in that email and encrypted messenger apps like Telegram and Signal afforded a means of tapping back into the journalists' sources inside of Russia. Just four months after the farewell livestream from Moscow, TV Rain was back online with a fresh menu of offerings. And it could demonstrate that its exiled status afforded protection from the Kremlin. The channel's editor in chief, Tikhon Dzyadko, participated in a Zoom interview of Ukrainian president Volodymyr Zelensky along with Russian journalists still based in Russia. In the interview, Zelensky excoriated the Russian army for not picking up the dead bodies of its own fallen men: "Listen, even when a dog or a cat dies, people don't do this." Irate Russian government authorities ordered the in-Russia outlets not to publish the interview. But for TV Rain, no longer in Russia, the decree was meaningless. The Kremlin could only fume.

Two months after the relaunch, TV Rain received a gift to its audience inside of Russia: Putin's troop-mobilization order. "When mobilization knocked on their doors," it was as if ordinary Russians suddenly discovered the war, the veteran Russian journalist Vera Krichevskaya, a co-founder of the channel, a 5 percent shareholder, and a top manager, told me in a Zoom call from her home in London. And now Russians were hungry for information—for what state media wasn't telling them. "We started thinking how to talk to them, how to communicate with them," Krichevskaya said. "Our main message was, do whatever you can to bypass the mobilization." And toward this end, the station consulted lawyers and other experts and told its viewers how Russian men could minimize the risk of conscription. With this surge in interest, the network announced that its Russian-language YouTube channel had attracted 40 million "unique viewers." With the ban on its operations inside of Russia, TV Rain was not able to monetize this audience through paid subscriptions, advertising, or other means. Still, this level of viewership was orders of magnitude higher than the following the channel received in its pre-exile existence and was proof to the managers and the newsroom journalists that TV Rain was finding its voice in its new life abroad.

Krichevskaya, for one, felt more energized about TV Rain than she had at any point since its founding. Only a year after TV Rain's 2010 launch in Moscow, she had stepped away from the network she had helped create, over disenchantment with its insufficiently aggressive coverage of Putin and his team, as she saw it. An activist journalist at heart, "maybe the biggest moment of my life," she told me on Zoom, came in her late teenage years, when, with the Soviet Union collapsing, she produced with her young friends, "with our own hands," an independent newspaper in her native St. Petersburg. As was typical for Putin's exiles in the making, that intrepid venture displayed a rebellious spirit at odds with parental passivity. A schoolteacher, she recalled, once screamed at her merely for asking how to spell her father's Jewish name—Isaac—in Russian: "I know how to write only Russian names!" Yet when Vera, only seven years old at the time, related this distressing episode to her father and mother, they responded with an embarrassed silence, their eyes cast down to the floor. She had gone into exile long before the war—in 2014, amid the nationalistic fervor in

54   Russia on Putin's annexation of the Crimea. In leaving for the
UK with her two young sons, "I really wanted to disconnect
them both from Russia," she told me. "I didn't want them to have
their roots, their emotional roots, there." But now everyone at
TV Rain was in exile, the war had supplied clarity to the network's mission, and Krichevskaya was once again fully engaged
in operations.

Yet even as viewership rose, a fresh peril arose for TV
Rain—a crisis that threatened to extinguish the channel altogether. The trouble began with a broadcast by the channel's
anchor Alexey Korostelev on the TV Rain program *Here and
Now* (*Zdyes & Seychas*). Speaking live from the satellite stu-
dio in Tbilisi, Korostelev offered a plug for TV Rain's hotline.
The hotline was a means for the network to obtain information, from Russian families and anyone else in a position to
know, on conditions faced by Russian troops on the front lines
in Ukraine. Tips could be sent to a TV Rain email address or to
the channel's Telegram bot. Such tips, TV Rain figured, could
be used to expose the Russian military's failure to provide ade-
quate supplies, whether boots or blankets, for the troops. These
revelations could help stir discontent with the government, the
channel thought. Korostelev, though, seemed to suggest a different purpose to the hotline: "We hope that we can help many
service members, for example, with equipment and basic ame-
nities at the front."

That one word—"equipment"—caused a tempest. Some
listeners heard a call for weapons for undergunned Russian
troops in the trenches in Ukraine. The outcry was immediate. In Ukraine, the government's culture minister, Oleksandr
Tkachenko, fired off a post on Telegram: "When 'good Russians'

are helping 'bad Russians'—can the world understand finally that they are all the same?" In Latvia, the government's defense minister, Artis Pabriks, suggested that TV Rain return to Russia, the residency permits for its Latvian employees annulled. Latvia's State Security Service announced an investigation into the anchor's remarks. The chair of the Human Rights Commission of the Latvian parliament declared that it looked like a bad idea, after all, for the country to host Russian media outlets like TV Rain: "Whatever Russian media might say against Putin, it doesn't mean that they're friendly to us."

Did these critics truly believe that TV Rain—the outlet that had run the banned interview with Zelensky as well as a segment on "Crimes against humanity by Putin's army" in the Ukrainian city of Bucha—was no better than Kremlin tools like RT? The fusillade spoke to a seemingly intractable issue facing Russian journalists in exile in places like Latvia. Some post-Soviet countries, and Latvia was a prime case in point, had constructed their new national identities, in part, on a foundation of anti-Russian sentiment. There were plenty of legitimate grievances, not least the invasion of Latvia in 1940 by the Red Army followed by the country's forced incorporation into the Soviet Union and the deportation of thousands of Latvians to prison camps in Siberia. Now, "de-Russification" was official policy, as could be seen in state efforts to expunge the study of the Russian language from schools. With Latvian tempers inflamed by the war, not much of a prompt was needed to target TV Rain.

Indeed, this was the most serious but not the first scrape between Latvian authorities and TV Rain. As absurd as it seemed to TV Rain, a chronic source of tension came down to a matter

56   of pronouns. Latvian authorities demanded that the network, with its base on Latvian soil, function as a Latvian company— so that news presenters would refer to Russians as "they" and Russian institutions as "their." But as TV Rain saw the issue, the channel, owned by Russians in exile, had an umbilical connection to the Russian audience back in Russia and its journalists could not differentiate themselves from their core audience. To live and work in Latvia did not make them Latvians. This dispute could not be resolved, and Latvian regulators fined TV Rain $10,000 Euros, in part for the offense of using the phrase "our army" for the Russian armed forces.

Now, Latvia's furious response to Korostelev's appeal for "equipment" for Russian troops drove TV Rain's alarmed management into hasty action: Just ninety minutes after Latvian defense minister Pabrik threatened to expel TV Rain from Latvia, the channel announced that Korostelev had been fired. Editor-in-chief Dzyadko said the "blunder" could not be tolerated in the midst of a war. But this executive decision provoked dismay among the rank and file in the TV Rain shop and also among the network's supporters in the Russian exile community. The abrupt termination of the anchor's employment was a misguided attempt, in their mind, to appease the Latvian government over an offense that did not merit such harsh punishment. Korostelev's fellow anchor in Tbilisi, Vladimir Romensky, handed in his resignation, and in this demonstration of support for his colleague, he was joined by two other TV Rain journalists. The firing was a "monstrous mistake" by management, Romensky wrote on Telegram. "They threw one of their own under the bus. They sent a loved one to slaughter. I can't do that, I'm gone."

The Latvian government, in any event, proved unappeas-
able. Five days after Korostelev's remarks on *Here and Now*, regulators revoked TV Rain's license on the basis that the channel
posed a "threat to national security and the public order." TV
Rain had to cease operations in Latvia immediately, and not only
that, stripped of its license, the network could no longer provide its offerings to cable providers anywhere. In Moscow, the
Kremlin exulted over the news: "All the time it seems to someone that somewhere is better than at home, and all the time it
seems to someone that there is freedom somewhere, but not
freedom at home," Putin's press secretary, Dmitry Peskov, chor-
tled. "This is one of the clearest examples that demonstrates the
fallacy of such illusions."

Amid this crossfire, TV Rain backpedaled. CEO Sindeyeva
told *Meduza*, an independent online news outlet run by Russian
exiles in Riga, that she regretted the firing of Korostelev: "We
were acting emotionally ... to us, it [was] like a complete
nightmare coming from all sides, and everybody would turn
their backs on us—Ukrainians, Latvians. . . . Which, in fact,
they did. . . . Of course, people shouldn't be fired for mistakes—
and we all knew that was a mistake. We could have taken him off
the air, stopped, thought about it." From London, Krichevskaya
told the *New York Times* that TV Rain had "left Russia to continue showing the reality of Russia's war to Russian people." But
now, she commiserated, "we are left without a territory. We have
no rights in Russia and we have no rights in Europe."

I met with Romensky at his hillside Tbilisi apartment a few
days after he had handed in his resignation in solidarity with
Korostelev and just hours after Latvian officials announced the
cancellation of TV Rain's license. He lived in Tbilisi with his

58   girlfriend, Marfa Smirnova, also a TV Rain journalist. It was late in the evening and the two looked drained. Seated at the dining table, Romensky hand-rolled a cigarette, pausing to take pulls from a bottle of beer, as he tried to explain to me, or perhaps to himself, why he continued to labor at reporting the news to Russians back in his native land as the strains of this task only intensified. "I can't be not Russian," he said in his fluent English, a torturous formulation that seemed to suggest he was an unwilling hostage to his national identity.

He then launched a mournful monologue that echoed Krichevskaya's lament to the *Times*. Where, he wondered, could TV Rain sink its roots? In Georgia, the government had just denied entrance to a Russian friend who was an anti-Kremlin activist. Under the prevailing attitude that "all Russians are bad guys," he noted, Georgian authorities could act just as the Latvians had done in expelling TV Rain: "We might be next." He loved Georgia, he added, yet understood, always, that "I am here as a guest."

Born in Moscow in 1987, Romensky told me he felt inspired to embark on a career in journalism by the example of Echo of Moscow, the pioneering independent radio station that was now also in exile, in Berlin. In 2015, when the opposition politician Boris Nemtsov was murdered on a Moscow bridge a short walk from the Kremlin's walls, Romensky was on the scene for TV Rain. The channel, at risk to its reporters, had faithfully covered any number of street protests demanding a "Russia without Putin." But maybe, he now told me, state media had won its propaganda campaigns. The Russian people, "they are really zombies," he declared.

It was not possible, I pushed back, to reach them? "There is
no way," Smirnova, joining the conversation for the first time,
agreed. But at her stark pronouncement, her boyfriend retreated
from what he had just said: "I think our work is to try to wake up
these people. . . . My grandfather is a robot. I think I can save my
grandmother." And Smirnova, too, took back her words. She dis-
closed that she was immersed in a project to speak with Russian
soldiers who committed atrocities in Bucha and now, in hopes
of lenience, were prepared to give testimony at war crimes trials at The Hague. As I took my leave of the pair, Romensky
whipped out his phone and with an impish grin showed me a
photograph he had taken of graffiti in Tbilisi: "Fuck Putin, not
Russians." And now that management had admitted that firing
Korostelev was a mistake, Romensky said he would take back
his resignation.

As it turned out, the blow dealt to TV Rain by Latvian
authorities, while severe, did not prove fatal. Five weeks later,
the channel announced that regulators in the Netherlands had
granted TV Rain a European broadcast license, good for five
years. This meant that TV Rain could return to cable networks,
its only source of revenue other than private donations, given its
inability to monetize its Russian audience. The channel would
now make Amsterdam the center of its editorial operations, as
soon as its staff received permission from Dutch authorities to
work and live there. As for fresh content, the network touted
its premiere of *Fascism in Modern Russia*, a film by the Russian
journalist Konstantin Goldenzweig on "the story of Germany's
descent into fascism in the 1930s, drawing parallels between
Germany back then and Russia today." TV Rain also announced

60 "a new episode of our hit satirical program, *Fake News*, which provides an insight into the bewildering, terrifying, and often farcical world of Russian State Propaganda." From its new home, the channel would be able to remain true to its root conception of itself as inseparably part of the Russian community, from wherever it was based. Score one over the Latvian government.

As the example of TV Rain suggested, the Russian news outlets operating from abroad were generally succeeding in their quest to offer Russians at home alternatives to state-controlled media. In the war's first several months, Roskomnadzor, the Russian government's regulator of mass media, blocked some ninety-five sources of "undesirable" information. But blocks on platforms like Facebook and WhatsApp could be evaded by the use of Virtual Private Networks (VPNs). And through popular, unblocked platforms, not only YouTube but also Telegram, Russians had access to an enormous variety of information from non-state outlets. Five months into the invasion, the total number of subscribers to the Telegram channels of independent Russian media outlets, virtually all of these outlets based outside of Russia, increased from 2.5 million to 4.7 million. The number of regular readers of Riga-based *Meduza*, for example, rose over this period by more than 150 percent, to 1.3 million, on the outlet's three Telegram channels. "Banned in Russia but here for you," *Meduza* told its readers. "The Real Russia. Today." As for YouTube, viewership over these first months of the war of the dozen principal Russian media and blogger channels on the platform increased by an average of 43 percent. These numbers represented a striking accomplishment for the outlets in exile.

The main problem faced by all of these outlets was not access to viewers and readers in Russia but a reliable means of financing their operations. On this dimension, the outlets were vastly outmatched. The Kremlin's pet outlets—from the RT network to the pervasive Rossiya-1, the flagship of the All-Russian State Television and Radio Broadcasting Company—drew on state coffers. Their budgets were effectively limitless. The news organizations in exile were unable to harvest advertisers, subscribers, or other possible revenue sources in Russia. For the most part they depended on charity—donations from sympathetic individuals of means and grants from philanthropic nonprofits. *Meduza*, deemed a criminal organization by Russian authorities, took contributions in not only dollars and Euros but also cryptocurrencies, which by their hidden nature allowed a giver to mask the geographic location of the donation.

There was, though, at least one deep-pocketed actor that spied a self-interest in assisting the anti-Putin information resistance: Washington. Some Russian journalists in exile received grants from the US Russia Foundation in Washington and Radio Free Europe / Radio Liberty in Prague, both groups funded by the US government. Such support was minuscule, no doubt, in comparison to the billions of dollars of US aid to the Ukrainian military to thwart Russia's invasion. But the purpose sprang from the same root understanding of this conflict as "a battle between democracy and autocracy, between liberty and repression," in the unequivocal terms of President Joe Biden. "While I have to draw a hard line on commenting on any of our grantees, I can tell you that we strongly support the work that Russian independent media are doing to reestablish their operations and preserve their audiences after involuntary exile from Russia in the wake of Putin's attack on Ukraine and massive increase in domestic repression," Matthew Rojansky, president of the US Russia Foundation, told me. He declined to disclose how many such projects the foundation was funding and the total amount of the grants. Both of the US government–financed projects I learned of on my own, in Tbilisi, were modest in scope. One supported an experienced Russian filmmaker developing a documentary on the deep poverty experienced by a remote town in Russia, the residents lacking reliable sources of water and heat. The other backed a married Russian couple with experience in television journalism who drew on freelancers back in Russia to place, on Telegram and other platforms, stories like local burials of Russian soldiers killed in the Ukraine war. Whatever the total amount of funding for all such projects, Washington was not a permanent solution for exiled journalists struggling to sustain themselves.

Aware that many Russians, especially in the younger generations, got their news and commentary from sources outside of the Kremlin's orbit, Putin's team of necessity paid close attention to the Russian outlets in exile. The two sides were locked in an acrimonious battle, in parallel to the shooting war in Ukraine, and this information combat had no foreseeable end other than, in the ardent aspiration of the exiles, the fall of the Putin regime. The hatreds were sincerely felt on both sides and no quarter would be given. "Their main weapon is propaganda," TV Rain's Krichevskaya sardonically told me of the Kremlin, "and it works better than their missiles." On this fluid battlefield, TV Rain expected that the Kremlin, sooner or later, would block YouTube. But the network, Krichevskaya told me,

was developing an app that would provide an alternative way to
deliver its content. "Very soon we will have our first release," she
said of the app, "and for us it is important to produce it before
they block YouTube."

The ingenuity of TV Rain—of all the exiled media—was
impressive. Yet the hard question remained: To what effect?
What impact did the burgeoning information resistance
have on the attitudes of the Russian public? A survey by the
well-respected Levada Center in Russia nine months into the
war found that 80 percent of Russians were "concerned about
the current state of events in Ukraine," with 42 percent "very
concerned." Some of those concerned undoubtedly thought
that Putin was too soft in his prosecution of the war—a criticism that hawks often registered on their own Telegram channels. Still, anti-war voices like TV Rain and *Meduza* surely
deserved credit for stoking worries about the war, especially
since 53 percent of those polled said they would rather "proceed
to negotiations" than "continue military actions." In a closed
Kremlin-commissioned poll around this time, the results
leaked to *Meduza*, only 25 percent said they favored a continua-
tion of the war over peace negotiations.

Yet 74 percent of Russians in the Levada Center's poll
answered yes to the question of whether they "personally support the actions of Russian military forces in Ukraine." And 81
percent expressed approval for the "activities" of Putin as president. The Levada Center conducted the survey by interviews
in the homes of Russians in urban and rural areas. It was certainly possible, at a time when it remained a crime to call the
"special military operation" a war, that some of the respon-
dents were afraid to reveal their real feelings about the war and

64   its champion. Nevertheless, the survey pointed to the immense challenge the information resistance faced in persuading the Russian public to reject the Kremlin-driven media line. In particular, "zombies" or not, older-generation Russians, who were raised on Soviet-era state television and who tended to embrace Putin as a traditional Russian strongman, acting as needed to maintain civic order, remained largely in the Kremlin's camp.

Ex–TV Rain anchor Alexey Korostelev, in a conversation in Tbilisi shortly after the network fired him, told me the channel needed to think beyond snagging a "positive reception" from those who already agreed with its perspective. "We need to construct a dialogue with the majority of Russians," he said. And toward this end, he added, it wasn't enough to carve out an anti-war identity: More coverage was needed on issues like the everyday economic concerns of the people. This struck me as sound advice, but I wasn't sure TV Rain would follow it, given that "no to war" was at the heart of its decision to bolt Russia and its sense of purpose in exile. Then again, all of the exiled outlets, trying to adapt to their unplanned new lives under harried conditions, were works in progress. For the information resistance, it was early days.

Warriors in Exile
"This Guy Stole Our Country"

Baby-faced, with a full head of brown hair and a wispy beard, Mikhail Kokorich looked younger to me than his forty-six years. Eight months into the war in Ukraine, we were meeting for the first time on Zoom. "I am from many nationalities," he told me, citing his Mongolian, Polish, and Jewish ancestry. Still, he stressed, he was raised "in the Russian culture. It's my language. It's my way of thinking." Kokorich was born in 1976 in Aginskoye, a settlement in easternmost Siberia just north of Russia's border with Mongolia. His mother and father separated just after his birth and from infancy he lived with his maternal grandparents. His grandfather was a school principal and his grandmother a teacher of physics and mathematics, and they instilled in him a love for books. He read widely, and not only Tolstoy and Dostoevsky, but also Jack London and Mark Twain. His home at times lacked electricity and, in the evenings, he read by the light of a kerosene lamp. It was from this early encounter with literature of many varieties that he traced the roots of an abiding political and philosophical identification

66   with Western liberalism. His first love, though, was for physics
and math, and there he excelled. The Soviet Union featured academic competitions for schoolchildren known as Olympiads,
and Mikhail consistently won first prize up to the regional
level in physics and math as well as in chemistry and biology.
In 1991, when he was turning fifteen, the USSR on the brink of
collapse, he took first place in the Russian national Olympiad
in physics and he repeated that triumph for the two years following. With his evident gift, he won an invitation to a boarding school in Siberia renowned for its physics and math studies,
and from there he gained admission to the physics department
of Novosibirsk State University, a premier training ground for
Russian physicists.

Most Russians felt frightened and disoriented by the spi-
raling chaos of the post-Soviet 1990s, as state-owned facto-
ries collapsed and public school teachers sometimes had to go
without pay. But Kokorich experienced this decade, stretching from his mid-teenage years to his early twenties, as a "nice
kind of anarchy," as he told me in one of our several lengthy conversations on Zoom. Amid the wreckage, he felt free to do as
he chose. In 1997, in the third year of his physics studies, his
degree unfinished, he decided to leave the university and try his
fortunes as an entrepreneur in the treacherous, yet for some,
lucrative domain of Russian business. And there he succeeded.
His first triumph had nothing to do with science: He founded a
home-goods retail store in a town outside of Novosibirsk and
assembled a chain of thirty-five outlets.

Yet even as he gained a profitable foothold in the Russian
business world, Kokorich was drawn to the emerging political
battles of the Putin years. "I hated the KGB—as a physicist, we

never liked these people," he told me. He joined Open Russia, a civic group founded by the magnate Mikhail Khodorkovsky, aimed at spreading liberal Western values to Russia's regions. And behind his convictions he put his wallet: On moving to Moscow, in 2008, he became a prime sponsor of a new anti-Putin political party, the money coming from the sale of his shares in his retail chain. He also contributed to a committee organizing street protests against the Kremlin's falsification of national elections. These were the typical activities of a Putin opponent with a bankroll, but Kokorich stood out for the radicalism of his beliefs. In his view, Russia was too big to be run out of Moscow—the real problem, of which Putin's control-oriented regime was a characteristic manifestation, was overcentralization. This analysis led him to embrace the improbable cause of Siberian independence, to be achieved, somehow, by peaceful means. Few people in Russia were talking about such a drastic step, but Kokorich, never afraid to be separate from the pack, was determined to put it on the agenda. He touted his opinion in conversations in political circles and, taking an appreciable personal risk, committed his advocacy of "Siberian separatism" to paper. "Large countries are behind the times of the modern world," he wrote in an article. "As an independent country, Siberia will have all the preconditions to be a truly democratic, pro-European and pro-USA state." Sure enough, the piece earned him a visit from Russia's security services. If he had not been on their watch list already, he was now.

By the time of Russia's invasion of Ukraine, he was in exile in Lausanne, Switzerland. His big idea sounded Elon Musk—like, to build hydrogen-powered "hyperplanes" with a range of 22,000 kilometers, capable of transporting passengers from

68   Tokyo to Brussels in two hours at a speed of Mach 6. The war,
      though, seized his immediate attention. He reached out to a
      friend in Switzerland, a fellow physicist, Alexey Boyarsky, a
      Kyiv-born Ukrainian who had studied at the prestigious Moscow
      Institute of Physics and Technology in the late 1980s and 1990s
      and who was now a professor of theoretical physics at Leiden
      University in the Netherlands. Boyarsky was also a researcher at
      the Swiss-based European Organization for Nuclear Research,
      known as CERN. As the Russian invaders threatened to over-
      run Ukraine, the pair turned their minds to an acute problem:
      the country's inadequate air defenses. Russian-launched cruise
      missiles, blind to Ukraine radar because the missiles flew so low,
      were inflicting massive damage on crowded apartment buildings
      and other civilian structures. So, too, were Russian-launched
      attack drones. With radar of no help, the need was for an alterna-
      tive means of detecting the cruise missiles and drones.

         The solution the two gravitated toward focused on acous-
      tics. Cruise missiles and drones emitted distinctive noises that
      could be picked up by noise sensors. With a sufficient number
      of these sensors—microphones, basically—placed on cell tow-
      ers and similar fixed structures on land, the sound vibrations
      recorded by the sensors and converted to electronic signals for
      wireless transmission could be used to determine the speed and
      flight path of the low-flying missiles and drones. Once fixed, the
      route could be relayed to the Ukrainian military, for the inter-
      ception and destruction of the approaching weapons before
      they smashed into their targets.

         As a physicist, Boyarsky on his own could work out the
      algorithm for calculating the trajectories of cruise missiles and
      drones. But he lacked practical experience in moving from paper

to actual production of the system he was designing. For this crucial part of the project, Kokorich's help was invaluable. In a Zoom conversation from Switzerland in which Kokorich participated, Boyarsky extolled his buddy's seemingly inexhaustible fund of energy and ideas from "day one," the day the war started. "Misha," Boyarsky told me, in the use of an affectionate diminutive for Mikhail, "was a better friend for Ukraine than many Ukrainians."

The first task was the development of a prototype. Anticipating that thousands of sensors would need to be manufactured, Boyarsky and Kokorich were determined to use cheap, off-the-shelf parts. Assembly could be done in Kyiv, with the help of physics students of Boyarsky. Placement of the noise sensors on cell towers and the like could be performed by Ukrainian utility companies. Kokorich contributed his own money to help finance the project and Boyarsky found other investors elsewhere. Boyarsky was the point of contact with the Ukrainian military and worked directly with the head of air defense for the Kyiv area.

Seven months into the war, the noise-sensor system was ready for wide-scale deployment. When I spoke with Boyarsky, the system had been up and running for about three months. He told me that it had been responsible for as many as two hundred detections of Russian cruise missiles and drones. He knew for sure that fifteen missiles had been destroyed by the Ukrainians as a result of the system, he said, and probably that many drones. Almost certainly the lives of Ukrainian civilians had been saved as a result of the efforts of Kokorich and Boyarsky.

Thirty minutes into my first Zoom meeting with Kokorich, when I learned of his war-related exploits, he unveiled a surprise:

70   a certificate of award—a *gramota*—bestowed on him by the
Armed Forces of Ukraine, known as the ZSU. "Thank you," the
document he displayed on the screen read, for "your continued
support and multiple contributions to the ZSU and Ukrainian
nation in their fight for freedom and independence of Ukraine."
At the bottom was the signature of Oleksandr Gruzevich, deputy chief of staff of Ukraine's ground forces. His theatri-
cal show of the *gramota* startled me—at the time, I knew of no
such awards—and the scene, which I recorded on tape, stayed
with me. I noticed on review that his emotional register, until
that point in our conversation fairly placid, suddenly changed,
as a grin swept across his face. He couldn't help from chuck-
ling too, as he talked about his achievement. My sense was that
he was exhibiting the pride any inventor might take in a suc-
cessful venture, but, more than that, a feeling of glee for best-
ing his nemesis, Putin, at the blood sport of war. For twenty
years he had opposed Putin, but his efforts had been largely an
exercise in futility. Now, with his tangible assistance to Putin's
enemy, Ukraine, he had the pleasure of long-delayed gratifica-
tion. "It's my war," he said of his clash with Putin. "It's my war,"
he repeated, "because this is our work of twenty years. It's personal. This guy stole our country."

Kokorich was not alone in his strivings as a warrior in exile.
For a hard-core, radicalized element in the Russian diaspora,
it was not enough to inveigh in words against the Kremlin, to
participate in anti-war street protests in outposts like Yerevan.
The overriding imperative was to assist the Ukrainian military
in its war against invading Russian troops. Russia's defeat, this
thinking went, was the surest and quickest path to a post-Putin
future. Their activities took a variety of forms—there was even

a unit of Russian volunteers pitted in direct combat against
Russian ground forces in Ukraine. Not since the Russian Civil
War of one hundred years before, fought between Bolshevik
and anti-Bolshevik forces, had Russians waged mortal combat
against each other. (Except in efforts by Moscow to quash sepa-
ratist insurgencies, as in post-Soviet Chechnya.)

Did the warriors in exile, I wondered, share certain traits
of character? Perhaps it was a case of an anti-type. A certain
trope depicted the Russian people as essentially conform-
ist in nature. Conformism, in this familiar view, operated as
a defense mechanism that enabled the masses to adjust to
autocratic political environments in which free thinking was
too exhausting. The by-product was passivity. "Conformism
of this kind is the basis of the Putin regime," a Russian pollster pronounced twenty-one years into Putin's rule. Yet a climate of conformism was also bound to breed, though in much
smaller numbers, opposites—the type that rejected herd
thinking and passivity. Those willing to cross over into active
support for the Ukrainian war cause struck me as contrarians
and free thinkers in the extreme.

They were also fearless, as their activities, as they well
knew, made them prime targets for Putin's wide-roaming and
ruthless security services. But as Kokorich told me, quoting
a folk saying in his native Siberia, "If you are afraid of wolves,
don't go into the forest." They wrestled, too, with questions of
ethics—the lengths to which they felt they could properly go
in helping the Ukrainians take on the Russians. Suppose, I said
to Kokorich, that Ukraine prevailed in the war, that Putin fell,
and that the Russian people, on learning of his support for the
Ukrainian side, blamed him for the death of their boys in battle.

72 "I am not helping Ukrainians to kill Russians. I am helping to defend them—to defend the people, the civilians," he replied.

Yet his Ukrainian friend Boyarsky confirmed for me something I had heard separately from an exiled Russian: that some exiles were assisting the Ukrainian military in procuring and producing attack drones that could be used to destroy targets like Russian tanks in Ukraine as well as to strike targets, like military airports, deep inside of Russia. Boyarsky told me that he personally knew of as many as forty Russians involved in various projects to help the Ukrainian military. "I know many Russian people," he said, who "really think that Russian soldiers in Ukraine have to be killed. There is no other way and they have no pity for them."

Nearly one year into the war, Ukrainian forces had managed on several occasions to strike military bases inside of Russia with combat drones, with apparent damage to military planes at a base in the Ryazan region about 125 miles southeast of Moscow. More such attacks could be expected. Over Zoom, I spoke with a wealthy Russian in Europe who told me he had given plenty of money to Russian political activist groups and Russian media outlets opposed to Putin. But on top of this, he had provided "small money"—about $300,000—to the Ukrainian military for the procurement of attack drones. He explained his reasoning in cost-benefit terms: A Russian tank costing millions of dollars to make could be destroyed by a single $20,000 drone. Support for the Ukrainian military is "the most efficient way" to bring down Putin's regime, he had concluded.

For Russian exiles with a taste for actual combat, there was a chance to join the Free Russia Legion, a unit of Russian soldiers fighting under the umbrella of Ukraine's International

Legion, a force that also included volunteer units of Americans, British, and Georgians. Ukraine formed the Russian unit six months into the war with the repeal of a law that barred Russian citizens from fighting alongside Ukrainians. It was not an easy matter for would-be Russian fighters to make it into Ukraine. On my visit to Yerevan, ten months into the war, a source with extensive contacts in that city's exiled Russian community told me that she knew of exiles who had flown to Moldova with the intention of crossing the border into Ukraine to fight against Russian troops. But they were thwarted, she said, by Moldovan authorities. My source also said that Russian intelligence officers in Yerevan, in order to learn how transit might be arranged, sometimes posed as exiles seeking passage to Ukraine to fight there against Russian soldiers. Still, some Russians outwitted the security services, as in one who left his home in St. Petersburg and enlisted in the Free Russia Legion. "A real Russian man doesn't engage in such an aggressive war, won't rape children, kill women and elderly people," this warrior, who went by the military call sign of Caesar, told a *New York Times* reporter in Ukraine. "That's why I don't have remorse," Caesar said. "I do my job and I've killed a lot of them"—soldiers of the Russian Armed Forces.

The Russian government's Prosecutor General's Office branded the legion a "terrorist organization" with "the aim of undermining the foundations of the constitutional system of the Russian Federation." The Ukrainian government, in turn, praised the fighters as heroes. "There was a large number of Russians who because of their moral principles could not remain indifferent and were searching for a way to enter the ranks of the defenders of Ukraine," a spokesperson for

74 Ukrainian military intelligence told the *Times.* "All legion-naires have come with a huge desire to stop Putin's horde and free Russia from dictatorship," he said. (Not all of the Russians in the Legion had left Russia to join the battle, though; some already resided in Ukraine when the war started.) With wealthy Russian exiles willing to help the Ukrainian military procure attack drones, it struck me as plausible, even likely, that such people were helping to finance Russian boys like Caesar seeking to join the Free Russia Legion. Through Boyarsky, I reached out to the Ukrainian military with a range of questions on support by Russian exiles for the Ukrainian war cause. How many Russians were involved in such activities? How many, in addition to Kokorich, had received awards? What difference to the war effort had such support made? Boyarsky said he would forward my questions to his contacts in the Ukrainian military but months passed without a response.

Still other Russian exiles directed their attention, not to the needs and capabilities of the Ukrainian military, but to opportunities to sabotage supply lines within Russia, to keep military resources from reaching the battlefield in Ukraine. In Yerevan, I met Andrei, a nineteen-year-old exile who casually informed me that he used his meager earnings as a motorbike delivery boy to donate, in cryptocurrency, to an anarchist group inside of Russia that carried out operations to damage Russian military railways. That sounded like a possibly fanciful story, but he referred me to the Anarcho-Communists Combat Organization, known as BOAK/ACCO, the group's website boasting of its exploits and providing a link for donations by means of a bitcoin wallet. "The cell of Anarcho-Communists Combat Organization in Vladimir claims responsibility for the sabotage action on the railway of military unit 55443 VD Barsovo," declared one such post, filed five months into the Russian invasion of Ukraine. The supposed site of the act, in a forest in the Vladimir region, was about sixty miles northeast of Moscow. An accompanying photograph showed the group's scrawled insignia on a length of disabled railroad track. A few weeks later, *Vice* used this photograph for a piece, based on interviews with a BOAK spokesman and other sources, that described how camouflaged saboteurs spent several hours "unscrewing dozens of nuts off the rails, and four off the rail joint, while keeping the electrical signal largely intact with a wire to evade detection." In a manifesto posted on its Telegram channel, BOAK said the defeat of Russia in the war in Ukraine "will increase the likelihood of people waking up" to "Putin's tyranny." Concerned about Putin's safety on the rails, his security team reportedly arranged for him to travel in a custom-built armored car and on a secret railway network.

His eyes shining, his words gushing forth, Andrei described himself as a committed "anti-fascist" anarchist in total dedication to the battle against Putin's regime and its war, to the point that he would be willing to take a gun and fight against Russian troops in Ukraine. Professing no fear of Russian security service operatives on the prowl in Yerevan, he wrote down for me his family name and allowed me to take his photograph. (I have no interest in speeding what may well turn out to be his path to prison somewhere, so am choosing to withhold his family name.) His backstory had one point in common with Kokorich's personal history: Andrei, too, was from Siberia, and also had lived for a time in Novosibirsk. In his seventeenth year, he moved with his parents to Turkey. But five months into Russia's

76   war with Ukraine, he took leave of his family and headed off, on his own, for Armenia. He had heard that there was a large Russian anti-war community in Yerevan. "My parents are very cowardly" in privately opposing the invasion but refusing to speak out, he told me—"that's why I left." Yet again, I had stumbled across a young Russian whose exile had taken the shape of an implacable familial rebellion.

In accounting for his beliefs and for his radical posture, Andrei began by citing the influence of Mikhail Bakunin, the nineteenth-century Russian anarchist and agitator who spent much of his life in exile in Europe. "The passion for destruction is also a creative passion," Bakunin famously wrote. An Italian anarchist also was an influence, he continued, and among the Russians, he cited Tolstoy and Dostoevsky along with the exiled twentieth-century philosopher Nikolai Berdyaev. (In his declaration at the outset of his tract, *The Russian Idea,* published in 1947, Berdyaev seemed to describe a type like Andrei: "The Russians have not been given to moderation and they have readily gone to extremes," he wrote.) I wondered whether his knowledge was broad but thin—he was not yet twenty, after all—but at the mention of Dostoevsky, we took a dive into the Grand Inquisitor chapter in *The Brothers Karamazov,* and it was plain that he had not only read this lengthy passage but spent time reflecting on its meaning. Andrei was a classic autodidact, a self-taught person attempting to apply imbibed knowledge to lessons for life. "Thanks to Tolstoy," he told me, "I quit tobacco, alcohol, meat, and sex. I get pleasure from platonic love." I found it hard to believe that his abstemiousness would endure. As Andrei surely knew, Tolstoy adopted an ascetic regimen late in life, a season of youthful wantonness long spent.

Andrei was plainly an exotic character. But what other kind of character sends cryptocurrency to a fringe sabotage group? There were others like Andrei out there, trading messages on Telegram and agitating for violent action to bring down Putin. He offered to introduce me to Russian exiles "in our movement," including an "anarcho-feminist" in Tbilisi. I was game, but we couldn't work out a good time for an in-person meeting. When the anarchists aren't issuing manifestos on Telegram or YouTube, they are busy trying to make ends meet with mundane jobs.

No doubt, many Russian exiles, probably a majority, wanted nothing to do with activities of any kind in support of Ukraine's war cause. "I am not going to take personal responsibility for a single life that could be lost because I facilitated this loss," an exile in London, active in humanitarian relief for Ukraine, told me. From Paris, Sergei Guriev told me he regarded Putin's army as "evil." Yet, "I don't want to kill just anybody. So I won't do that, whatever I think of Putin and his army." As to "who's correct and who's not—it's a very difficult conversation," he added. Guriev served with Kokorich and other prominent Russian exiles on what was known as the Anti-War Committee, a group formed after the invasion of Ukraine. "It was not the Russians who started this war, but a mad dictator. But it is our civic duty to do everything we can to stop it," committee members declared in a joint statement. But the committee took no official position on support for the Ukrainian military. That was for individual members to decide on their own, as Kokorich had done.

Still, the longer the war continued, the greater the destruction meted out by Russian forces, surely the numbers of actively engaged militants among the exiles would grow. After all, a general spirit of combativeness already seemed to pervade the Russian exile community. Boris Akunin, in exile in Europe, was one of the world's most popular writers in the Russian language; his mysteries had sold many millions of copies in Russia. He was also a belligerent opponent of Russia's military campaign in Ukraine. In an email exchange, I asked him what he had to say to the Russian boys on the front lines. He sent back a message to the troops, his ire focused on the masterminds of the war in the Kremlin: "Those imbeciles gave you weapons. Excellent. You are armed now. Do the right thing, turn your weapons against those who stole your freedom, who started this absurd war. They are your real enemies, not Ukrainians."

An armed uprising against Putin still seemed a dream, even though the aborted Prigozhin mutiny in June 2023 briefly raised this possibility. Yet dreams could be their own form of sustenance. As I considered what might bind Andrei and Kokorich, a professed anarchist and a serial entrepreneur, beyond their shared traits as contrarians and free thinkers, perhaps the answer was a strain of millenarianism. In the Christian Bible, millenarianism finds expression in the idea that an apocalypse on earth, wrought by God, can usher in the second coming of Christ. But this sort of thinking can crop up in secular guise, nourished by the faith or simply the desperate hope that a catastrophe like a war could be followed by a better, a more just, order of things. Andrei longed for the abolition of private property. Kokorich had his cherished vision of independence for Siberia—and that day, he believed, might yet come.

The Spiritual Resistance
"My Faith Is Optimistic"

"I am not a political activist," Father Oleg Batov, a priest of the Russian Orthodox Church, was explaining to me. We were having a light lunch at a café in Batumi. On a December day, ten months into the war, sunlight poured through the glass panes as we gazed out at the placid waters of the Black Sea. With his mane of white hair and a long flowing beard, Batov looked like an Orthodox priest. But he was dressed in an open-necked shirt and jeans, not in the traditional black cassock of the Orthodox clergy. On deciding to flee Moscow shortly after the war began, Batov chose Batumi for its mild climate—and also because he hoped a church there would permit him to preside over services. And for one month following his arrival, he was able to celebrate the rites. But then he received a visit from a bishop of the Georgian Orthodox Church, who told him he had to stop. The bishop, Batov explained to me, was acting out of a desire to preserve good relations with Russian Orthodox Church leaders in Moscow, whose support for Putin and the war Batov had challenged. Now Batov earned what money he could by driving a taxi and offering his services as a tour guide.

His wife, Maria—Russian Orthodox priests are permitted to marry—joined us at the café, along with the couple's teenage son. A metal cross dangled from a loop around her neck. Maria was helping to support the family with private music lessons— vocal and piano—to adults and children and with jazz and rock gigs at Batumi restaurants. This turn in their lives was quite a comedown for both Oleg and Maria. In Moscow, Oleg had presided over the sixteenth-century Church of the Assumption of the Blessed Virgin, a minute's walk from the Kremlin. Years earlier, he had headed a Russian Orthodox church in Zurich, visited at that time by the wife of Putin's protégé Dmitry Medvedev. Maria was an accomplished musicologist, a graduate of the Moscow State Tchaikovsky Conservatory who had performed with the Boston Camerata, the renowned early-music ensemble. But the pair evinced no regrets over their decision to flee Russia. Because of the war, it was "just impossible" to remain, Oleg told me. "In our heart we are Christians," he said, and God's commandment was unambiguous: "Thou shalt not kill." He was not a political activist, by his self-description, but he surely was a kind of spiritual rebel against the powers-that-be in his native land, including the leadership of his own church.

The saga of the Batovs might sound strange to the Western ear. Apart from the Kremlin, no institution in Russia was as reviled in the West as the Russian Orthodox Church. Prominent secular voices in the Russian exile community in Europe widely shared this loathing. On one level, this was understandable. The Church seemed to stand for a mystical sort of Russian imperialism. This outlook was embodied in the organization's reigning leader: His Holiness Patriarch Kirill of Moscow and All Rus'. Six years older than Putin, Kirill was enthroned in 2009, nine years into the Putin era, and together the Patriarch and Russia's Tsar-like ruler displayed a harmony of purpose and vision. In particular, they subscribed to a concept known as *Russky Mir*—Russian World—which held that a distinct Russian Orthodox civilization, built up over a millennium, extended seamlessly across national boundaries into places like Ukraine. The Russian-peopled lands, in that way of thinking, could be justly reclaimed by the Russian state. In this lens, Russia's annexation of Crimea in 2014 represented no mere territorial enlargement, but the return of sacred ground: In the Russian origin story, Prince Vladimir converted to Orthodoxy with his baptism at an ancient site in Crimea and "then christened the whole of Rus'." Following the annexation, the *Russky Mir* project advanced with the Kremlin-fomented military insurgency in Eastern Ukraine aimed at bringing the Donbas region, inhabited by many ethnic Russians, under effective Russian state control.

In 2020, Kirill consecrated a massive new cathedral—The Main Cathedral of the Russian Armed Forces—that symbolized the fusion of the military and religious spheres in a resurgent post-Soviet Russia under Putin's command. Erected on the site of a military theme park on the outskirts of Moscow, the structure featured frescoes that celebrated Russian martial triumphs from medieval to present times and a floor that was fashioned from melted-down weapons seized from Nazis. A mosaic was created for Putin, but taken down after he said it was too early to memorialize his accomplishments. Two years later, the Russian invasion of Ukraine now entering its second

82   month, Kirill returned to the cathedral and spoke to the "faithful" on the war. "All of our people today must wake up, wake up,
understand that a special time has come, on which the historical fate of our people may depend," he said. "I do not cease to feel
anxiety for all the people who live in those places where military clashes are taking place today," he continued, speaking of
Ukraine. "After all, all these are the people and peoples of Holy
Rus', all these are our brothers and sisters. But, as in the Middle
Ages, wishing to weaken Rus', various forces pushed the brothers against each other, plunging them into internecine strife, so
it is happening today." By "various forces," the Patriarch seemed
to be calling out the West, as in the US, the EU, and NATO, as
the real instigator of the Ukrainian conflict. And in response to
the West's troublemaking, he concluded, "we must be faithful—
when I say 'we,' I mean, first of all, military personnel—to our
oath and readiness to 'lay down our lives for our friends,' as the
word of God testifies."

Putin could not have asked for a more resounding justifi-
cation for the war. Yet for all the attention that the Putin-Kirill
alliance garnered in the Western press, there was a larger context
that the media tended to neglect. Although Kirill was elected to
his position as Patriarch in a secret ballot of an electoral body
composed of clergy and laypeople, he was not the equivalent
of a Roman Catholic Pope as an infallible source of divine wisdom. The world of Orthodoxy, which included other national
churches, had no Pope. And the Russian Orthodox Church itself
was bigger than its Patriarch and his political and cultural fixa-
tions. *Russky Mir* was not Church dogma and had nothing to do
with the Gospels.

The story of the Batovs and their eventual flight from Russia offers a window into the messy realities of Russian Orthodoxy—a complex, layered institution that was not as homogeneous as it appeared from the outside. Inside the Church, familiar tendencies like cultural chauvinism and attachment to autocracy often prevailed but not without challenge from countervailing currents like ecumenicalism and a populist suspicion of state power. The question of what the Church was—and what it could be—was a live one, at the core of an abiding struggle deep within its ranks that dated to Soviet times and came to a head in the late 1980s as Soviet-imposed strictures on religious worship loosened. The Batovs were part of that struggle, as advocates for an outward-looking, "people's" Church, as opposed to an institution bent on inculcating a strong sense of Russian nationhood and on aligning with the state. In exile, along with like-minded others in the Church who had fled Russia, they represented a fledgling spiritual resistance to Kirill, their pushback grounded in Christian principles. They represented, too, hope for a reformed institution that, in a post-Kirill, post-Putin society, would fulfill their vision of what the Church must stand for to engage the hearts and minds of the laity without misty appeals to imperial dreams.

Oleg was born in 1969 in Moscow. His father, an electrician, died when he was a small child, and he was raised by his mom, a kindergarten teacher. "I had a common Soviet education and upbringing," he told me, of no religious content, apart from household rituals like making *paska*, the traditional Russian Easter bread. He entered into the study of physics at the Moscow Engineering Physics Institute and seemed bound

84   for a career in science. But at the age of nineteen, for the first time, he opened a Bible. As unexceptionable as that act might seem, the Bible was officially banned by the state for much of the Soviet era, available only through the clandestine *samizdat* (self-publishing) strivings of dissidents. But now, as publishing restrictions eased in Mikhail Gorbachev's USSR, a French publisher brought out a million copies of the New Testament in Russian, and a curious Oleg purchased one. Even as he continued with his physics studies, he hungered to know more about religion and began to attend free lectures in Moscow on the history of Christianity.

Maria came to belief even earlier than Oleg. Born in 1970 in the ancient Russia city of Novgorod, a few hundred miles northwest of Moscow, her father was a jazz pianist and her mother a journalist. At the age of sixteen, she entered a college to study as a musicologist and there on the syllabus was Bach's *St. Matthew Passion*. "I think God found me through what I loved the most— music," she told me. "Bach's music reveals the Gospel like nothing else." At home, her mother gave her a copy of the Gospel of Matthew in a black handwritten book—copied by her mom at the age of twenty-five, when she managed to borrow a copy of the Bible for twenty-four hours. Maria received her baptism at this time, in 1986, and on that day put on the cross I saw on her in Batumi. She wore it always.

Of inspiration to both Maria and Oleg in coming to Christianity was Alexander Men, a charismatic priest "for a new generation of believers," as an acolyte described him. Born in 1935 to a Jewish family, Men was baptized as an infant in the Catacomb Church, a branch of the Russian Orthodox Church that spurned cooperation with Soviet officialdom.

Under Stalin and his successors, the Church, such as it was permitted to exist in cramped form, was under constant watch by the KGB and many priests had reputations as KGB informers. As a threat to this collaboration between Church and State, Men suffered constant KGB harassment. Nevertheless, he persisted in his teachings, to the point of holding underground Bible classes. Possessed of a wide-ranging intellect and an encyclopedic knowledge, he situated Christ in a stream of moral instructions that ranged from Plato to Moses, Muhammad to the Buddha. And he took Marx, the high priest of Stalinist-Leninist Communism, to task for the famous aphorism that "religion is the opium of the people." Not in the least, Men said in a lecture: "For those Christians who might be tempted to turn their faith into an easy chair, a refuge, a tranquil harbor, Marx's formula is a warning! No, Christianity is not a security blanket." Instead, he continued, "Authentic Christianity is, if you wish, a mountain-climbing expedition, a dangerous and difficult undertaking."

Men's was a Gospel of direct action, of engagement with the world beyond the walls of a formal house of worship, and he brought his ministry directly to the poor and the sick. With the arrival of *glasnost,* with Soviet dogma at last exposed as bankrupt, his time seemed to have come. Word of mouth swelled his following. Captivated by his ideas and example, Maria arranged for a lecture by Men at her musical college. Yet, as she well knew, "many were against Men within the Church," opposed to his "open," outward-looking viewpoint, as she recalled in our conversation in Batumi. On a Sunday in September 1990, as he made his way from his home along a path to the train station to get to his parish church in a town outside of Moscow, he was

86   attacked from behind, a blow to his head from an axe draining his blood and ending his life. The axe, the traditional tool of the Russian peasant, suggested, perhaps, a symbolic message, that the killing was by the hands of Russia. Was this the work of right-wing nationalists? The KGB? It looked in any event like a professional operation by a team that had closely observed Men's routine and carefully plotted the assault; no culprit was ever brought to justice.

Now Men was a martyr, a body of writings and a committed circle of followers left behind. Unlike Maria, Oleg did not have a chance to meet Men before the priest was murdered, but he had read his works and attended talks offered by Men's associates. With the dissolution of the Soviet Union, Men's central lesson, that "the Church should serve people, not the authorities," as Oleg took it, had a chance for enactment. For this "new generation of believers," projects like the restoration of long-abandoned churches nourished the hope that Russian Orthodoxy could be rebuilt on a new foundation, close to the laypeople, separate and apart from the state. On graduating from his physics institute, Oleg enrolled, one year later, in a theological institute. He met Maria in 1993 at a small Gospel reading and prayer group in Moscow, in the tradition of such groups founded by Men in his lifetime, when preaching was not permitted in churches. They were married that year.

In the post-Soviet 1990s, Orthodoxy enjoyed a resurgence in popularity among laypeople and became a badge of fashion in certain political and business circles. Boris Yeltsin announced that he was now a believer after his many years as a "sincere atheist" in Soviet times. Church leaders doubted Yeltsin's vow of faith and saw him as a weak, undisciplined ruler. No matter:

Patriarch Alexei II, the predecessor of Kirill, enthroned in 1990, forged a pact with the Russian Armed Forces that revived Tsarist-era practices like religious instruction to teach fresh recruits to serve "God and Fatherland" and ecclesiastical awards for generals. In the ebb and flow within the Church, the stalwart conservative faction, seeking a close bond with the State, was ascending over the populist, ecumenical camp stirred by the teachings of Alexander Men. And on Putin becoming president, "patriotic Orthodoxy" blossomed into a kind of state ideology, a replacement for the "scientific atheism" that the KGB itself had once embraced. The Kremlin started a pro-Putin Orthodox youth movement, known as Walking Together. Strange stories made the rounds in Moscow, as in a top Putin aide vetting candidates for appointments to federal office for Orthodox belief and even asking if they would mind being baptized. Putin himself said his mother had him secretly baptized; some experts in Orthodox rituals said his body language in church passed their test for a genuine believer. Five years into Putin's reign, I met in Moscow with the priest said to be Putin's personal confessor. He lavished praised on Putin as the first true Christian head of state since the last Tsar, Nicholas II, and as the protector of the national soul—the *pervoye litso* (first face)—of Russia, as tradition assigned this role.

Yet as Putin increasingly took on the cast of the Tsars of old, with approval from Church "statists," voices of dissent within its ranks arose. In 2012, a dozen years into Putin's reign, amid the street protests in Moscow over election fraud, I spoke with a young seminarian who professed sympathy for the demonstrators. "Power has to be based on moral values that serve the people. It shouldn't be a power that dominates people," he said. And

88   in this regard, he continued, the "more often the young generation stands up for its rights, the more often the government
will take into account the opinion of the young people and of the
country." An anti-Putin opposition gradually took shape inside
the Church. In 2019, as political protesters again took to the
streets, ninety-four priests signed an open letter calling on the
government to halt criminal prosecutions of protesters. Father
Batov was the top name on the list. In a piece published by the
Moscow Times, a photograph of him in his church placed at the
top of the article, he declared that, as St. Augustine taught, "a
state devoid of justice is no better than a band of robbers."

Two years later, Oleg tried in vain to convince Russian
legal authorities not to shut down the Memorial group, the
nonprofit devoted to chronicling the crimes of the Soviet
Gulag. He was becoming dangerously close to being seen as an
enemy of the state by Putin's Kremlin. Nonetheless, six days
after Russia's invasion of Ukraine, he joined with nearly three
hundred Orthodox priests in signing an open letter calling
for an "immediate ceasefire" and saying the Ukrainian people
should be permitted a free choice, "not at gunpoint," to deter-
mine their relationship with Russia. Furious at this breach,
security service operatives summoned some of the signatories
to the Lubyanka, in Soviet times the fearsome headquarters
of the KGB, now occupied by its principal successor agency.
The rebellious priests were pressured to remove their names
from the letter. Oleg was not among those summoned, but he
understood how carefully he had to watch his words. In a ser-
mon at his church, he awkwardly refrained from calling the war
a war. Meanwhile, the director of Maria's musical conservatory

signed a letter in support of the invasion. It was in these untenable circumstances that Oleg and Maria concluded that they had no alternative but to flee the country. Oleg wrote a letter to his parishioners explaining that as he could no longer keep silent on the war, he felt he had to go into exile. The missive was read aloud in his church. "Most understood, some were saddened, some were hurt," he told me. Maria notified her conservatory of her resignation on arriving in Batumi. She rejected, categorically, the idea that Putin was a sincere believer: He has yet to perform "any Christian deeds befitting a president," she told me.

Oleg was among a fairly small number of Russian Orthodox priests who went into exile after the Ukraine invasion. But many more clerics pined to leave Russia, I was told by Sergei Chapnin, a fellow priest and a friend of Oleg's, in exile in America. The two met in the mid-1990s as colleagues in the Office of the Moscow Patriarch. Chapnin, who rose to become the editor of the main publications of the Church, was now the leading point of contact for disaffected priests inside and outside of Russia. He was the one who directed me to Oleg. Alexander Men, too, was an inspiration for Chapnin, and a "people's Church" perspective could be seen in the criticisms of Kirill's tenure that Chapnin regularly published on a website, Public Orthodoxy, sponsored by Fordham University in the US. He spoke to me on Zoom from a friend's house on Long Island. On the wall behind him was a print of the famous Andrei Rublev icon of the Holy Trinity. Chapnin told me that "frightened" priests in Russia, privately unaccepting of Kirill's embrace of the war, called him "quite often" to speak of their desire to go into exile. The

90   problem, Chapnin said, was that the Church leadership could
      suspend or even defrock them—and thus make it impossible
      to be accepted by Orthodox churches outside of Russia. They
      would have to reinvent their lives and they faced dim prospects,
      unlike the readily employable IT workers who had fled Russia.

      Chapnin well understood the predicament—he faced it
      himself, as did Oleg Batov, halted from preaching in Batumi—
      but his patience was running out. He was especially exasper-
      ated with the bishops of the Church for parroting Kirill's line,
      and not only that, for refusing to let the parish priests under
      their domain to voice opposition to the war. With the war near-
      ing its one-year anniversary, he posted on Public Orthodoxy
      an accusatory letter addressed to the bishops, titled "Why
      Have You Forgotten the Truth of God?" The years of Kirill's
      rule, he told them, "are dark pages in the Church's history. The
      Church's renaissance broke down, and now it is not sinners
      being saved by divine grace who are its members, but embit-
      tered castle-builders swilling the cocktail of imperial myth,
      resentment, and unbelievably primitive eschatology." You are
      the drinkers of this foul cocktail concocted by Kirill, Chapnin
      told the bishops, and what's more, "in a great many photos you
      are there, next to the patriarch, smiling, receiving his blessing,
      offering him flowers and expensive gifts. Once again: You stand
      by a man who justifies war crimes and has betrayed the Church.
      You repeat his words, retell his criminal arguments."

      In his missive, Chapnin acknowledged that "I myself am in a
      weak and vulnerable position. The reproach that may be thrown
      at me is obvious: 'You left Russia, you are now safe, do you have
      a moral right to utter these reproaches?'" Still, he asked the
      bishops, "Who prevents you from leaving, too?" If any of you

inwardly disagree with Kirill, Chapnin wrote, but "see the risks and threats connected with the free manifestation of your position," then "leave, just as hundreds of thousands of Russian citizens have left. Many of them are Orthodox; they need priests and bishops. They wait for free preaching, for spiritual support. Remember that after the October revolution, dozens of bishops left Russia and established Russian churches outside Russia, and now not a single one of you has done the same."

It was a remarkable screed—to what effect, it was hard to say. Fordham's Public Orthodoxy website was blocked in Russia by state authorities, but an in-Russia site, ahilla.ru, published Chapnin's letter, and translated versions were published in Polish, Bulgarian, French, and German. "As far as I know," Chapnin told me, "quite a few" bishops read it. His project for the long term, he said, was nothing less than the reformation of the Church. It needed to be "radically reorganized," he said. And the "first thing" was that "the Church would be clearly, totally separated from the State." Second, the parishes, "now totally in the hands of the bishops," would need to have "much greater autonomy." In this decentralized setup, "the parish should be recognized as the main entity of the church." And to sever altogether the ancient bond between the Church and political autocracy, Chapnin favored turning Russia into a parliamentary republic, shorn of a separately elected president. His dream was that "Christian democrats" could be a "political force" in this Russia.

There was no chance, of course, of a reformation of the Church under Kirill, seventy-six years old and apparently in good health, notwithstanding a bout with COVID. And there was no historical precedent for a radical reorganization of the

Russian Orthodox Church. But these were not the only obstacles facing embattled reformers like Chapnin. Another was that voices like his were just about alone in the wider Russian exile community. The discussion of Russia's future was almost entirely a secular one. "True Russia," a group composed of prominent exiles belonging to the "Russian cultural world," promoted a secular, European-oriented conception of Russia that would survive Putin. The group's website featured high-profile writers like Boris Akunin, a founder, and accomplished musicians like the conductor Vladimir Jurowski, but so far as I could see, no religious figures of any affiliation. "We are humanists," True Russia's managing director, Oleg Radzinsky, told me in a Zoom call from London. Radzinsky was a writer and financier who had spent more than three years in a maximum-security prison in Soviet times on conviction of charges of "anti-Soviet agitation and propaganda." True Russia, he said, stood for "the Russia of Pushkin, not the Russia of Putin."

The ubiquitous Guriev was also a founder of "True Russia." He was not engaged with religious issues, he told me from Paris, and in any case, he suggested, "Russia is not a very religious country." Yet while fewer than 10 percent of Russians attended church regularly, the share of Russians identifying as Orthodox Christian surged after the collapse of the Soviet Union, from 31 percent in 1991 to 72 percent in 2008, according to a Pew Research Center analysis of data from social scientists. Another Pew survey, conducted from 2015 to 2017 in thirty-four countries, found that 75 percent of Russians believed in God, compared to 36 percent of Swedes. A 2021 survey by a Russian research outfit and the University of Oslo found that 47 percent

of Russians supported "mandatory study of Orthodox culture"
in primary schools.

These findings suggested that religious belief and institutions were also part of a true Russia. Indeed, the spiritual resistance mounted by Church clerics like Chapnin and Oleg Batov to the Putin-Kirill alliance was of the same character as the anti-Putin resistance in secular exile circles, even as that shared perspective went generally unacknowledged by secular leaders. The believers in the diaspora had defied the Kremlin, just like the nonbelievers, in refusing to embrace Russia's war. On top of that, the believers had disobeyed the Patriarch of their Church, in rejecting his framing of the war as an existential struggle on which the "historical fate" of Russia depended. All of those who fled were equally "scum and traitors" in Putin's eye. In this context, the apparent absence of coordination between the secular political and spiritual resistance to Putin and the war struck me as a missed opportunity.

On taking leave of Maria and Oleg Bartov in Batumi, I asked Oleg whether he could see himself returning to Russia and resuming his activities as a priest. "I would love to," he told me—on the condition that Putin was no longer in power. A people's Church, he felt, could yet be built, "without golden steeples and gilded icons." Even in these dark times he refused to succumb to despair: "My knowledge is pessimistic. My faith is optimistic." That saying, he noted with a smile, came from Alexander Men.

Waiting for Navalny
"The Fact Is I Am a Christian"

He gazed out on us, the piercing blue eyes conveying, as ever, an intensity of purpose. An image of Alexei Navalny was on display on a large screen set before a packed house in an auditorium on the campus of New York University in Manhattan. At this particular moment, eight months into the war in Ukraine, the man himself resided in a prison colony in Russia. The occasion was the award to Navalny, in absentia, of the Civil Courage Prize, given by the New York—based Train Foundation "to those who fight tyranny as a personal mission." Alexander Solzhenitsyn was the original inspiration for these annual prizes. In opening remarks, Mikhail Baryshnikov, the former ballet star who defected from Soviet Russia in the 1970s, cited Navalny's demonstrated willingness to sacrifice himself for the cause of making Russia a democracy: "He loves Russia and its people more than anything else."

Navalny could be thought of as Putin's most important exile—in the sense that the banished political prisoner is a traditional Russian form of exile, practiced in Tsarist and

Soviet times and revived in the Putin era. Confined in solitary to a small room, he was awakened by guards at six in the morning, his cot then chained upright to a wall, a lone backless stool to sit on. He was permitted one book, and for thirty-five minutes of the day, pen and paper. All this *after* Russia's security services had tried to kill him with a nerve agent on a trip to Siberia, a clumsily executed operation later exposed by Navalny himself. He nearly died from the poison, but recovered in a German hospital—and then chose to return to Russia to face a certain prison sentence on dubious charges he stole money from his own group. "Alexei Navalny is not a saint," Michael McFaul, the former US ambassador to Russia, said in a short film tribute played at the Train Foundation gathering. "He is human." But that disclaimer only seemed to underscore the otherworldly arc Navalny seemed to be tracing in his remarkable saga.

Even from a prison cell, Navalny was the Kremlin's most confounding and intractable opponent. A Navalny organization, operating in his name and able at times to receive his instructions from intermediaries, remained at work with a headquarters office in Vilnius of about seventy people and loyal activists in exile elsewhere in former Soviet Republics, in Europe, and even in North America. Wealthy Russian exiles contributed money to the Navalny group, formally known as the Anti-Corruption Foundation, and lieutenants conducted fundraising drives to supplement these funds. What was more, the organization had an extensive network of contacts inside of Russia. No other Putin opponent could rival these active links to loyalists in cities and small towns spread throughout the vast country.

Navalny's seemingly unique status in the anti-Putin opposition was not just a matter of his personal sacrifices. His
admirers and even his persistent critics in anti-Putin circles attested to his charisma and his wiles. Born in 1976 in a
rural area outside of Moscow, the son of an army communications officer, he studied law and finance before turning to
politics with a sharp focus on shady state-business transac-
tions he had a knack for documenting. He rose in prominence
a decade into Putin's rule, a young man in his mid-thirties, on
fire with condemnation of Putin's regime as a gang of "crooks
and thieves." Anti-Putin, Western-oriented Russian liberals,
though, viewed the Navalny of this period with suspicion: They
saw him as more of a populist demagogue than a European-style
democratic leader. In one widely seen video, he expressly
backed the deportation of Central Asian migrants, many of
whom were Muslims. In another video, a call for gun rights, he
took pistol in hand and "shot" shadowy figures from Russia's
Muslim-populated Caucasus region—individuals he likened
to cockroaches and flies. Nevertheless, Navalny's core focus on
corruption resonated with large numbers of ordinary Russians.
They agreed that sleaze motivated by greed was a defining feature of not only Putin's hold on power but also the grip exerted
by Kremlin-subservient officials throughout Russia. Navalny's
messaging was brilliant, and as everyone who met him said, he
could command a room.

          As I peered into the Navalny organization and spoke with
friends who had known him for years, with donors to the outfit and committed field activists, as well as with his critics, I
considered its prospects in the treacherous world of Russian
exile politics. Jealousies and rivalries abounded in this murky

universe, where personal egos and ambitions threatened to undermine cooperation between like-minded figures. I wondered, too, about the caliber of the people Navalny had put in charge of his organization while he was confined to prison. What kind of leadership did they exhibit? That question was hardly an idle one, with the Navalny team intent on shaping the future of a post-Putin Russia. Like all good revolutionaries, they thought not just of the hour of triumph but of the hour after the hour of triumph. Their expectation was for a vicious scrum to follow Putin's demise, as occurred after Stalin's death in the early 1950s, and they aimed to be on top.

On hand in New York to accept the Civil Courage Prize on Navalny's behalf were the two most important people in his organization: Leonid Volkov, his chief of staff and chair of the Anti-Corruption Foundation, and Maria Pevchikh, head of the foundation's investigative division. Volkov was born in 1980 in a factory town in Russia's Ural Mountains region, his mother a professor of information technology and his father of mathematics, his parents compromising "a classic example of the Soviet scientific-technical intelligentsia," in the son's words. Leonid concentrated on math, at one point attending school in Dresden. He was drawn to the IT sector in his late teenage years, and by his mid-twenties he was managing projects with hundreds of employees reporting to him. An interest in politics, though, won out over his business pursuits, and at the age of twenty-eight he won election to the Yekaterinburg city council. There he caught the attention of Navalny, always on the lookout for promising talent in Russia's regions, and with his city council term to expire, Volkov moved to Moscow to work for Navalny.

On the surface, he had the profile of a manager-technocrat, whether applying his skills to the business or the political sector. "Digital freedoms," he liked to say, could protect Russia "from its irresponsible politicians." But there was more to Volkov than a narrow focus on scientific methods. Born into an ethnically Jewish family that disavowed traditional religious faith, he turned to Judaism in his thirties and along with his wife became an observant practitioner of the religion. Judaism, he felt, offered an "integrated moral-ethical system" compatible with science and modern life. At times expressing himself in Hebrew, he told *Tablet*, the New York—based magazine of Jewish affairs, of his enjoyment in keeping Shabbat and other rituals. In that piece, published one month before Putin's invasion of Ukraine, he also flashed impatience with the reporter's suggestion that his boss had failed to disavow the rancid nationalistic videos made years before. He conceded that Navalny's chauvinistic comments were "very unpleasant to watch now," but added that Russians had already forgotten them: "The Russian voter has the memory of a goldfish."

Short, stocky, and rumpled, Volkov had a large head equipped with a reddish-tinged beard that begged to be described as Lenin-esque. He was famously brusque. At the New York event, I approached him with a request to meet with him at his Vilnius headquarters for the book. He was prepared for my entreaty, as a colleague had already briefed him on my interest in learning more about the Navalny organization from the inside. "We are not interested in being part of this project," he replied, the "we" seeming to speak for the entire Navalny organization. Startled, I asked why not, and he repeated his words without elaboration. I related this brief encounter to Sergei Guriev in Paris, and he did not seem surprised. He knew Volkov, as he knew just about everyone who mattered in the exile community, and on occasion visited the Vilnius offices to offer guidance to the staff. "I think there are many people who can teach him communications skills," Guriev said of Volkov. That was one of the milder comments I received on Navalny's chosen top manager. Everyone "hates" him, blurted an exile in Washington, DC, who was deeply immersed in anti-Putin projects. A more considered critique was ventured by a prominent Russian political figure in exile in Europe. This person, who asked not to be named in order not to jeopardize his relationships in exile political circles, including a personal friendship with Navalny, told me that Volkov had to be seen as a reflection of his boss. Just as Navalny was, "unfortunately," an "authoritarian politician," this figure said, Volkov was an "authoritarian manager." The main difficulty, my source continued, was that Volkov was intent on the Navalny organization being "the only political force" in the Russian exile community: "He doesn't want to collaborate with other political groups and politicians."

It was undoubtedly the case that the Navalny organization, under Volkov's stewardship, insisted on steering its own course and unapologetically so. Just over six months into the war, exiles filed into the ballrooms of the Grand Vilnius Resort for a three-day conclave billed as the first "Congress of Free Russia." The lead organizer was Garry Kasparov, the former world chess champion turned human-rights activist who had left Moscow for New York City in 2013. "The goal of the Congress is to unite the efforts of the most active anti-war elements of Russian society with those of their Western counterparts as we seek to build a global coalition in defense of Ukraine and against

100   Putin's regime," Kasparov said. Yet even as delegates met within easy reach of the Navalny team's offices in a duplex in a residential part of Vilnius, Volkov chose to stay away. "I don't know why they are doing these types of events," he told reporters. "Of course, we all want regime change in Russia. But we have our projects. . . . We don't believe that attending some conferences is helping this."

Still, even critics conceded Volkov's talents as a political strategist, and others in exile circles said Volkov was probably the right person to manage the Navalny organization given the circumstance of the founder serving a sentence of nine years in prison. "The chief of staff should be authoritarian, because he is in charge of the organization," Sergey Aleksashenko, a deputy finance minister in the Yeltsin years in Russia who now served on the Anti-war Committee, told me over Zoom from his home in Washington, DC. Aleksashenko had helped pay for Navalny's medical treatment to recover from the nerve-agent poisoning, he confirmed to me, "because we are friends." As for Volkov, "maybe he lacks some wide political vision and that's why the combination with Navalny was good," Aleksashenko said. "The best chief operating officer is maybe not the best chief executive officer," he noted. Still, Volkov "is very efficient, very pragmatic, he is able to deliver results."

In contrast to Volkov, Maria Pevchikh, in charge of the Navalny group's investigative team, was slim, elegant, and graciously mannered. But she was every bit as fierce. Pevchikh was born in 1987 in a town in the Moscow region. The daughter of a manager of a chain of hotels, she won a coveted place, at the age of fifteen, to study sociology at Moscow State University. But she was repelled by the corruption she found at the institution—"It was like $200 to pass an exam"—and moved to the United Kingdom to study at the London School of Economics. In her early twenties, back in Moscow, she applied for a position advertised on Navalny's blog for a person to study procurement contracts, and as she liked to tell the story, "He got back to me five minutes later with a joke saying that I had the perfect résumé of an MI6 spy." She plunged into the drudgery of poring through the UK land registry to spot deals involving Russian oligarchs. In time, the two paired on muckraking investigations that in sensational fashion exposed corruption at the highest levels of Russia's governing class. *Putin's Palace*, a nearly two-hour video on a $1.3 billion mega-mansion by the Black Sea, reputedly built for the Kremlin's leader with funds from oligarch cronies, was the single most popular video on Russian YouTube in 2021, drawing tens of millions of viewers. Street protests ignited in response to depictions of luxuries like a sub-terranean ice hockey rink and an enormous tea house for guests. "It's politics," Pevchikh told a *Guardian* reporter of such presentations, crafted to rouse "a very wide audience."

With Navalny away in prison, she affixed a poster of him—"Be scared of nothing," read the slogan—on her office wall in Vilnius. "I am just convinced, and I will fight anybody who will tell me that I'm wrong, I am *convinced* that Russia can be a normal, democratic, liberal country," she told the audience at the New York event. In a chat on the sidelines, she objected to my use of the word "exile" to describe people like herself. "I don't consider myself to be in exile. It's a sad word. I live in Russia." But while her mind may have resided in Russia, her foot had not touched ground there for two-and-a-half years, she acknowledged. "Don't waste your time trying to assign probabilities in a chaotic system" for the precise time of Putin's final day in power, she told the New York gathering. "Our job is actually to just be prepared" while "holding the seat warm" for Navalny. "I have a very clear instruction from my boss" to continue the organization's work, she said, "and I am following that very much."

Happily, for my sake, Volkov proved not be an especially effective "authoritarian" with regard to my project, as it was easy to get people connected to the organization to speak with me despite his royal pronouncement that "we" had no interest in cooperation. As I reflected on my impressions of his team and their implacable dedication to the cause, a phrase often used to describe the Irish Republican Army came to mind: "the Hard Men." The Navalny people were more battle tested, more seasoned, than most of the exiles I encountered. They had made an irrevocable choice: Each knew they faced prison on return to Russia, so long as Putin stayed in power, merely for an association, any tie, with the banned Navalny organization. As the truest of the true believers, they seemed impervious to the doubts that afflicted many exiles as to whether Russia would ever move past repressive rulers like Putin. A political mission had seemed to meld with a quasi-religious quest.

Their unwavering commitment to the cause came across to me in an encounter with Daniel, a Navalny activist I met in Yerevan. Daniel was among the group of the dozen-plus Russians who showed up for what I billed as a general discussion of life in exile. While he made no effort to dominate the conversation, it was plain he already had given thought to every question I tossed out, and afterward I asked to speak to him alone in a side room. As he stood up from his chair, the first thing that struck me was his physique: He stood six feet, six inches tall,

and was rail thin—a string bean. Sure enough, he had played
semi-professional basketball. He was from the Siberian town of
Omsk, born there in 1991, the month before the expiration of
the USSR. "I used to joke, I was born in the Soviet Union, but the
Soviet Union could not handle me," he told me with a wan smile.
His well-educated parents, his father an engineer, his mother a
physician, were "budgetnikov," he said, using the Russian word
for the class of people dependent on state salaries. This meant
they were "easily controlled" by the government, Daniel said.
But he was not, as in the case of other exiles I encountered, con-
sciously pitted against the example of his parents. He studied
engineering, dropped out of school, and took up a job refur-
bishing houses. His foray into political activism grew out of
personal financial troubles. He was doing well in his construc-
tion work until 2014, when the West sanctioned Russia for the
annexation of Crimea and money dried up in the economy. Until
then, he took no interest in political matters. But now he started
to read *Meduza* and to show up at anti-government protests.
Seeking a deeper involvement in the political arena, he joined
the Communist Party in Omsk, as the only organization that
seemed to be doing anything to oppose the Kremlin.

In 2017, the Navalny organization opened an office in Omsk
and Daniel took a course the Navalny team offered in election
monitoring. His ties with the Communist Party had never been
strong and when the Navalny office recruited him for a salaried
position on its professional staff, he accepted. He saw Navalny
frequently at this time and was impressed: "He explains difficult things in simple terms, so anyone can understand." And the
Navalny team's resolute focus on corruption as the essential
evil in Russia spoke to his own experience. "Corruption explains

104   everything that happens in Russia," Daniel told me. "Corruption
and authoritarianism are two sides of the same coin."

As it happened, Navalny, after being stricken with poison in the summer of 2020, was taken to a hospital in Omsk.
Daniel kept vigil outside the hospital with fellow Navalny supporters. In 2021, the Russian government forced the shutdown
of the Navalny organization in Russia. Now out of a job, Daniel
was slapped with a civil lawsuit claiming that he owed the state
two million rubles for government expenditures to protect the
public against unauthorized protests in which he had participated. Facing a sure defeat in court, he fled Russia shortly before
the invasion of Ukraine. From Yerevan he continued his political organizing work as best he could with his contacts in Siberia.
Unafraid to be identified, he provided me with his family name
and his contact on Signal and permitted me to take his photograph. Better for the Russian security services to expend their
energies on tracking him, he joked, than on chasing comrades in
Ukraine.

Daniel's loyalty to Navalny and the Navalny organization,
for all his trials, clearly was unshaken. He was a trained and
stress-tested foot soldier, just over thirty years old, ready and
waiting for whatever duty called. But was there really no person other than Navalny, no team other than the one he had put
together, capable of leading the struggle against Putin? Mikhail
Khodorkovsky and his London-headquartered organization
might have looked like a good fit for this role. Khodorkovsky had
a compelling story of personal suffering: Before Navalny, he was
"Russia's best-known prisoner," as America's National Public
Radio called him on his release from prison in 2013, a pardon
granted by Putin, a plane taking him to Germany. He had spent

ten years in confinement; the world had seen images of him in prison garb at a Siberian penal camp and had read of his periodic hunger strikes, including one to protest the denial of medical treatment to a gravely ill fellow inmate. "To some people, especially in the West, Khodorkovsky came to be viewed as a figure like Nelson Mandela, ennobled by suffering and ready to lead his country to a new kind of society," NPR said.

Ten years after leaving Russia, one year shy of sixty, Khodorkovsky devoted virtually all of his time and energy to anti-Putin opposition activities. From his base in London, he aired his views on his Russian-language YouTube channel, a kind of personal video blog, which in 2022, received 67 million views, according to numbers his spokesperson gave me. He promoted his book, *How Do You Slay a Dragon?*—a "manual for start-up revolutionaries," published in Russian, which offered his vision of a post-Putin future for Russia. His model was along the lines of the decentralized federalist system of Switzerland, in which state power was shared at the national, canton, and commune levels. "I know how to build a new structure for a new government," he told an interviewer for *Blick,* a Swiss publication, on the one-year anniversary of the Ukraine invasion. "Only a few in the opposition have experience with that." The magazine hailed him as "Putin's greatest Russian opponent."

But that was a distinctly Western view of Khodorkovsky. In the Russian perspective, the Mandela parallel was strained. Khodorkovsky had endured harsh prison punishment, but in the preceding chapter of his life, he had amassed enormous wealth in oil-company privatization deals greased by his close ties to Boris Yeltsin's government. He was a prime example of the oligarchs that became a hated class in post-Soviet Russia. By his

106 own admission back then, "political sponsorship" was crucial to his rise in the business world. Then, too, for all of his exertions from London, Khodorkovsky had not set foot in Russia since his 2013 pardon. "He has no connection to the Russian people—none," Sergei Guriev, who served with Khodorkovsky on the Anti-war Committee, told me. Khodorkovsky "tried to build" a political organization, including in his promotion of candidates for the Russian parliament, but "he failed," Sergey Aleksashenko, also on the Anti-war Committee, told me. "I would say Khodorkovsky is not charismatic as a political leader," Aleksashenko continued. "He is very clever, he is very good at discussions," but "people should be ready to join you. You should attract them by your ideas, by your words, by your actions. They should see you and trust you. And be ready to follow you." A third member of the Anti-war Committee disapprovingly likened Khodorkovsky to "a prime minister of a Soviet country. He has a plan for everyone."

These criticisms perhaps were shaped by partisanship for Navalny, "number one" as the face of the Putin opposition, in Guriev's clear-cut appraisal. Nevertheless, in all of my encounters with politically active Russian exiles in places like Yerevan and Tbilisi, no one volunteered Khodorkovsky's name as an opposition leader. He was "not a leader" but "a manager," I was told in a conversation in Tbilisi with an activist who had formerly served as the regional coordinator, in the Siberian town of Tyumen, of the Khodorkovsky-founded Open Russia group. Indeed, it was possible that whatever ambitions Khodorkovsky once held as a future leader of Russia, he had scaled them back. In his interview with *Blick*, he seemed to rule out running for elective office in a post-Putin Russia: "I am not a politician. I am an experienced manager who knows crisis management. Besides, I'll soon be sixty. I can no longer work fourteen-hour days, seven days a week."

Garry Kasparov, the promoter of the Congress of Free Russia, also was a member of the Anti-war Committee and he had a platform in the West as the author of opinion pieces like one for the *Wall Street Journal* on "Putin's Culture of Fear and Death." He shared his byline in a *Washington Post* op-ed with the Putin critic Michael McFaul, the former US ambassador to Russia. But from his home in New York, Kasparov, who turned sixty in 2023, lacked the organization the Navalny team had in Russia. Then there was Ilya Ponomarev, a self-proclaimed "left-libertarian anarchist" who was the sole member of the Russian parliament to vote against the annexation of Crimea. From his base in Kyiv, Ponomarev, now a Ukrainian citizen, founded a Russian-language channel, February Morning, which offered tips on bomb making in service of a call for a popular uprising against Putin. Ponomarev was an outspoken critic of Navalny: "He will not share power with anyone." But then, too, Ponomarev faulted both Khodorkovsky and Kasparov for staying out of Ukraine because they knew, he said, that such a visit would be unpopular with Russians back in Russia.

Such carping promised to be interminable and reminded of the constant feuds, a mixture of ideological and personality differences, among the "whites" who fled Russia after the Bolshevik seizure of power. The frictions broke the anti-Bolshevik diaspora into ever smaller fragments. The same dynamic was a threat to the anti-Putin movement. Still, even the volatile Ponomarev acknowledged Navalny as the "most powerful" Putin opponent. Seven months into the war, the *Washington Post* published under Navalny's name an opinion piece that set forth a vision of a post-Putin Russia: "The future model for Russia is not 'strong power' and a 'firm hand,' but harmony, agreement, and consideration of the interests of the whole society. Russia needs a parliamentary republic. That is the only way to stop the endless cycle of imperial authoritarianism." This new model, he made clear, was a replacement for the flawed "presidential republic" structure, with a weak legislative body, established on the dissolution of the Soviet Union, under which Yeltsin and then Putin ruled. The piece seemed designed to allay lingering concerns, including in Western capitals, that Navalny was a brute populist of an authoritarian stamp. Guriev told me that he and his wife, Ekaterina, had helped Navalny to craft the piece, long in development, before Navalny went to prison. "He has changed a lot—he has become much wiser," Guriev said. A 2022 book co-authored by Guriev, *Spin Dictators: The Changing Face of Tyranny in the 21st Century*, was among Navalny's requested readings in prison, Guriev mentioned to me.

The Oscar-winning documentary film *Navalny* kept his chilling story—"Poison Always Leaves a Trail," the promotion tag read—front and center to viewers of CNN and HBO Max. But how Navalny was regarded in American households, or by political elites in Washington, Paris, London, and Berlin, was not what mattered most to his prospects. First, his organization needed to keep its house in order. In March 2023, three days before *Navalny* won at the Oscars, and five months after Volkov and Pevchikh accepted the Civil Courage Prize at NYU on Navalny's behalf, a scandal surfaced. It emerged that Volkov, in the name of the Navalny Anti-Corruption Foundation, had appealed to the European Union's foreign policy chief to lift sanctions against several Russian oligarchs. Volkov was forced to acknowledge he had exceeded his personal authority in signing this appeal, and as a result, Pevchikh took over for him as the chair of the Anti-Corruption Foundation. Yet Volkov remained part of Navalny's team. "Volkov made a mistake" and "took the responsibility for it," an embarrassed Navalny said on social media. "All that has happened has been a good lesson for us."

Beyond maintaining the integrity of his organization, the most important objective for Navalny was keeping his standing with the Russian people. Navalny always had been acutely conscious of this precious bond. In his last opportunity to speak to Russians before going to prison, he displayed his striking ability to appeal to their hearts. "The fact is that I am a Christian," he declared in February 2021, in his "closing remarks" to a Moscow City Court considering his appeal of his prison sentence. This "fact," he said, "usually rather sets me up as an example for constant ridicule" in his organization, "because mostly our people are atheists and I was once quite a militant atheist myself. But now I am a believer." He proceeded to read from a letter a Russian man had sent him: "Navalny, why does everyone write to you, 'Hold on, don't give up, be patient, grit your teeth?' . . . The Bible says, 'Blessed are those who hunger and thirst for righteousness, for they will be satisfied.'" Just so, Navalny now told the court: "And I thought, how well this man understands me!"

Always one to tailor his self-presentation for maximum effect, Navalny made no mention in this peroration that the chief of staff of his team of "atheists" was an observant Jew. Still, his final court appearance struck me as a characteristically dazzling specimen of performance art. He was offering his saga of

110   personal suffering—his defining choice to endure further hard-
         ship in returning to Russia after recovering from his poison-
         ing in Europe—as a classic Christian parable, which indeed it
         was. And even more than that, he was presenting his unquench-
         able "thirst for righteousness" as a parable of Russia. His arc
         was Russia's arc, and Russia, as he told the court, deserved
         deliverance from "a vicious circle of unhappiness." No wonder
         Putin viewed him as a dire threat. But that didn't mean Navalny
         wasn't sincere in his conversion to Christianity. "He became a
         believer," Boris Zimin, a close Navalny friend, assured me in a
         Zoom call from Berlin. A wealthy philanthropist, Zimin at one
         point was the single largest donor to the Navalny organization,
         and he, too, helped pay for his friend's recovery from the poi-
         soning. In Zimin's telling, Navalny absorbed the Bible and the
         lessons of the Gospels, and his return to Russia, after nearly
         dying, was "a deep philosophical act." As the war ground on, as
         Navalny endured a kind of living martyrdom, it was hard not to
         think that his story remained unfinished.

              His story remains unfinished, as does the saga of Putin's
         exiles. Exile, as generations of Russians have discovered, is an
         indeterminate station in life. "As I look back on those years of
         exile," Vladimir Nabokov wrote in his memoir, *Speak Memory,*
         published in 1951, "I see myself, and thousands of other
         Russians, leading an odd but by no means unpleasant exis-
         tence, in material indigence and intellectual luxury, among per-
         fectly unimportant strangers, spectral Germans and Frenchmen
         in whose more-or-less illusory cities we, émigrés, happened
         to dwell." Eventually, of course, an end arrives. Never to return
         to his native land, Nabokov wandered around America and
         Europe and died peacefully in Switzerland in 1977, at the age of

seventy-eight. For the politically engaged, unrelenting in the struggle against the ruling power in Russia, the end could be ghastly: Leon Trotsky at his compound in Mexico City, an ice axe planted in his skull by an agent of Stalin. Yet some Russian exiles found fulfillment of their dreams, as in the case of Lenin in 1917 and, on the collapse of the Soviet Union some seventy years later, Solzhenitsyn. With the expiration of the "godless" empire he despised, he ended his eighteen years of rustic remove in the woods of Vermont and returned to a hero's welcome in Russia.

When will be the end for Putin's exiles? The ghastly already has been seen, as in the death of Alexander Litvinenko in a London hospital weeks after poisoning by radioactive polonium-210, the assassination of the former Russian security services officer "probably" approved by Putin, a British government inquiry found. Still, the lesson of exile movements is that they must be viewed with a long time frame. Their life cycle is typically measured in decades. The daily drama that plays out in newspapers and captures our eyes may not portend the final result. It's entirely possible that the generational rebellion of which Navalny is now the foremost leader will be taken over by someone younger than he is. For Putin's exiles, just maybe, triumph awaits.

I want to thank Nick Lemann, Jimmy So, Camille McDuffie, and Allie Finkel at Columbia Global Reports for their support, encouragement, advice, and most of all patience in bringing this book project to completion. Thanks to Leigh Grossman for the copy edit. In the field, I received help from Ivan Divilkovskiy and Darina Maiatskaia in Yerevan, Andrei Novikov in Tbilisi, and Timur Mukanov in Batumi. Sergei Guriev, Sergey Aleksashenko, Oleg Radzinsky, Vera Krichevskaya, Alexsei Fisun, Sergei Chapnin, Pietro Shakarian, Anastasia Burakova, Igor Zevelev, Masha Lvova, José Vergara, Oliver Ontiveros, Lara Setrakian, Marc Cooper, and Christian Caryl steered me to good contacts for interviews. Bernie Sucher, Leslie Starobin, Shlomo Segev, and Eran Segev were helpful sounding boards. My wife, Nargiza Yuldasheva, was both a wise source of advice and a rock of support—and it is to Nargiza this book is dedicated, with love.

This is the first book published on Russian exiles in the Putin era. For a broad understanding of the exile experience throughout history, *The Oxford Book of Exile* (Oxford University Press, 1995), edited by John Simpson, is an authoritative source. Alexander Herzen's *My Past and Thoughts* (University of California Press, 1982) is a classic account of a Russian exile's life in the nineteenth century. Leon Trotsky's *My Life* (Dover, 2007) devotes many of its pages to his efforts, while in exile, to wage revolution against the Tsarist regime. For the Russian experience of exile in the twentieth century up through the Soviet period, Michael Glenny and Norman Stone chronicle individual stories in *The Other Russia* (Faber and Faber, 1990). John Glad brings together interviews with prominent Russian writers in exile, conducted between 1978 and 1989, in *Conversations in Exile* (Duke University Press, 1993). Vladimir Nabokov's *Speak Memory* (First Vintage International Edition, 1989) is perhaps without peer as a literary reflection on a life in exile. Ivan Bunin's *The Twilight of Émigré Russia, 1934–1953* (Ivan R. Dee, 2002) is also worthwhile.

For an understanding of the currents of thoughts among Russians as a people, Nikolai Berdyaev's *The Russian Idea* (The Centenary Press, 1947) always rewards. As to Russia's pre-Soviet history, Geoffrey Hosking's *Russia: People and Empire* (Harvard University Press, 1997) is a useful single volume. For the Putin period, Mikhail Zygar's *All the Kremlin's Men* (PublicAffairs, 2016) is an indispensable guide to his court. Putin's rise to power and takeover of the commanding heights of the Russian economy are chronicled in Catherine Belton's

Putin's People (Farrar, Straus and Giroux, 2020). Fiona Hill and
Clifford G. Gaddy's *Mr. Putin* (The Brookings Institution, 2013)
is revealing of his operating style and methods. Masha Gessen's
Never Remember (Columbia Global Reports, 2018) grapples
with the erasure in Putin's reign of memory of the Gulag. The
rise of the Russian Orthodox Church in post-Soviet Russia
is told in John Garrard and Carol Garrard's *Russian Orthodoxy
Resurgent* (Princeton University Press, 2008). The Church's
growing involvement in Russia's armed forces is the focus
of Dmitry Adamsky's *Russia Nuclear Orthodoxy* (Stanford
University Press, 2019). *Religion During the Russian-Ukrainian
Conflict* (Routledge, 2020), edited by Elizabeth A. Clark and
Dmytro Vovk, is a valuable collection on an underappreciated
subject. Alexander Men's life, times, and philosophy are ren-
dered in Yves Hamant's biography *Alexander Men* (Oakwood
Publications, 1995). The sensibilities of Russians in the period
that began with the collapse of the Soviet Union are vividly
explored in Maxim Osipov's collection of short stories, *Rock,
Paper, Scissors* (New York Review Books, 2019).

NOTES

INTRODUCTION

13   jacket illustration: John Simpson, editor, *The Oxford Book of Exile* (Oxford University Press, 1995).

13   I met with: I conducted personal interviews with Russian exiles in Yerevan, Tbilisi, and Batumi in December 2022, and in some cases followed up with conversations on Zoom and exchanges on WhatsApp.

16   on a sealed train: Lenin's journey is recounted in https://www.therailwayhub.co.uk/11242/from-the-archive-by-train-to-the-revolution-the-journey-that-shook-the-20th-century/.

17   "restoration of sovereign power": On Sun Yat-sen and exiles in Japan, see https://taiwantoday.tw/news.php?unit=29,45&post=36812.

19   as many as one million Russians: Data on Russian exodus in the *Washington Post,* February 13, 2023, https://www.washingtonpost.com/world/2023/02/13/russia-diaspora-war-ukraine/.

20   "because my conscience": Letter quoted in https://canadiandimension.com/articles/view/the-blurred-reality-of-russian-patriotism.

20   "Liberalism in Russia is dead": Quoted in the *New York Times,* February 19, 2023, https://www.nytimes.com/2023/02/19/world/europe/ukraine-war-russia-putin.html.

21   "definitely" responsible: Survey cited in *Foreign Affairs,* February 1, 2023, https://www.foreignaffairs.com/ukraine/how-russians-learned-stop-worrying-and-love-war.

CHAPTER ONE: FLIGHT

26   by mid-March, some 300,000: A mid-March survey by OK Russians cited in the *Wall Street Journal,* April 10, 2022, https://www.wsj.com/articles/fleeing-putin-thousands-of-educated-russians-are-moving-abroad-11649583003.

28   two million "white" Russians: See https://www.rbth.com/history/333001-how-millions-of-russians-fled.

28   young German men: On German and Japanese men fleeing to avoid conscription, see https://www.eurasiareview.com/12032022-countless-men-have-emigrated-to-avoid-military-draft-many-came-to-america-oped/.

29   "It takes a strange mentality": Quoted in Roger Neville Williams, *The New Exiles* (Liveright Publishers, 1971), p. 321.

31 **"I'm sorry, we're from Moscow":** Quoted in the *New York Times,* January 15, 2003, https://www.nytimes.com/2023/01/15/world/asia/bali-indonesia-russians-ukrainians.html.

31 **"inappropriate to celebrate Russian music":** quoted in *First Things,* March 14, 2022, https://www.firstthings.com/web-exclusives/2022/03/the-cancellation-of-russian-culture.

31 **"I came to realize":** Quoted in the *New York Times,* November 28, 2022, https://www.nytimes.com/2022/11/28/us/russian-activists-asylum.html.

32 **improbable trek:** Story told in the *Washington Post,* October 20, 2022, https://www.washingtonpost.com/opinions/2022/10/20/russian-student-describes-fleeing-country/.

32 **an "underground railroad":** Network described in the *New York Times,* February 14, 2023, https://www.nytimes.com/2023/02/14/world/europe/russia-antiwar-dissidents-escape.html.

33 **"collective West" and "scum and traitors":** Putin's translated remarks in the *Moscow Times,* March 18, 2022, https://www.themoscowtimes.com/2022/03/18/putin-comments-on-the-fifth-column-a76987, and Fox News, March 17, 2022, https://

www.foxnews.com/world/putins-inhumanity-ukraine-self-purification-traitors.

33 **"a war criminal":** Quoted in Associated Press, April 5, 2023, https://apnews.com/article/russia-putin-defector-war-crimes-khodorkovsky-karakulov-dossier-845421fe06ed9cfa1962ad4f98a2e413.

33 **"illusory goals":** Pugacheva Instagram post quoted in the *New York Times,* September 18, 2022, https://www.nytimes.com/2022/09/18/world/europe/alla-pugacheva-ukraine.html.

33 **"We hate war":** From Osipov article in *The Atlantic,* May 16, 2022, https://www.theatlantic.com/books/archive/2022/05/russian-citizens-leaving-russia-ukraine-war/629859/.

34 **some 10 percent:** Cited in the *Washington Post,* February 13, 2023, https://www.washingtonpost.com/world/2023/02/13/russia-diaspora-war-ukraine/.

35 **"my daughter":** Quoted in the *Wall Street Journal,* February 26, 2023, https://www.wsj.com/articles/russian-women-flock-to-argentina-to-give-birth-b6e65569.

CHAPTER TWO: GUILT

37 **at least 100,000 Ukrainian soldiers:** Estimate by Gen. Mark

118 Milley, chairman, US Joint Chiefs of Staff, cited in BBC article, November 10, 2022, https://www.bbc.com/news/world-europe-63580372.

37 **credibly accused of rape and torture:** United Nations investigation finding that "war crimes have been committed in Ukraine" by Russian troops in NBC News, September 23, 2022, https://www.nbcnews.com/news/world/russian-troops-raped-tortured-children-ukraine-un-panel-says-rcna49168.

37 **reeducating the children:** In "Russia's Systematic Program for the Re-education & Adoption of Ukraine's Children," report by Yale School of Public Health, February 14, 2003, https://hub.conflictobservatory.org/portal/sharing/rest/content/items/97f919ccfe524d31a241b53ca44076b8/data.

39 **He left Russia in 2013:** Guriev's abrupt flight in the *New York Times,* May 29, 2013, https://www.nytimes.com/2013/05/30/world/europe/economist-sergei-guriev-leaves-russia-abruptly.html.

42 **"like an unexpected":** In Ivan Turgenev, *Diary of a Superfluous Man* (W. W. Norton, 1984), p. 20.

45 **"too intimate":** In Susan Neiman, *Learning from the Germans* (Farrar, Straus and Giroux, 2019), p. 8.

45 **"far more trusted":** Susan Neiman, *Learning from the Germans,* p. 374.

45 **"Prussian State":** Quoted in Jonathan Steinberg, *Bismarck* (Oxford University Press, 2011), p. 18.

46 **"false image":** Quoted in Reuters, October 07, 2022, https://www.reuters.com/world/memorial-chronicler-soviet-recent-crimes-banned-by-putin-2022-10-07/.

47 **"an 'expendable' territory":** In Nikolas K. Gvosdev, *Imperial Policies and Perspectives Towards Georgia, 1760–1819* (St. Martin's Press, 2020), p. 64.

CHAPTER THREE:
THE INFORMATION RESISTANCE

49 **"special military operation":** Putin used this language in his first pronouncement on the invasion. See Reuters, February 24, 2022, https://www.reuters.com/world/europe/russias-putin-authorises-military-operations-donbass-domestic-media-2022-02-24/.

49 **"spread panic":** Parliamentarian quoted in the *New York Times,* March 4, 2022, https://www.nytimes.com/2022/03/03/world/europe/russia-ukraine-propaganda-censorship.html.

49 **"wresting our people"**: Simonyan quoted in the *New York Times,* December 22, 2022, https://www.nytimes.com/live/2022/12/20/world/russia-ukraine-news.

50 **"No to war":** See the *New York Times,* March 4, 2022, https://www.nytimes.com/2022/03/03/world/europe/russia-ukraine-propaganda-censorship.html.

51 **"revolutionary journalism"**: Isaiah Berlin in his introduction to Herzen's memoirs, *My Past and Thoughts* (University of California Press, 1982), p. xxxi.

52 **"dog or a cat dies"**: Zelensky quoted in the *New York Times,* March 27, 2022, https://www.nytimes.com/2022/03/27/world/europe/russia-media-zelensky.html.

54 **"We hope that"**: Korostelev episode in *Meduza,* December 2, 2022, https://meduza.io/en/feature/2022/12/02/equipment-and-basic-amenities.

54 **"When 'good Russians'"**: Tkachenko Telegram post quoted in the *New York Times,* December 6, 2022, https://www.nytimes.com/2022/12/06/world/europe/ukraine-russia-war-latvia-tv-rain-journalism.html.

55 **"Whatever Russian media might":** Latvian official quoted in *Meduza,* December 2, 2022, https://meduza.io/en/feature/2022/12/02/equipment-and-basic-amenities.

55 **"Crimes against humanity"**: TV Rain news segment, September 28, 2022, at https://www.youtube.com/watch?v=YQDcb1yvMIw&ab_channel=TVRainNewsroom.

56 **Latvian regulators fined TV Rain:** Episode in *Radio Free Europe/Radio Liberty* article, December 2, 2022, https://www.rferl.org/a/russia-dozhd-tv-fined-latvia-licence/32159364.html.

56 **"monstrous mistake"**: Romensky Telegram post quoted in *Meduza,* December 3, 2022, https://meduza.io/en/news/2022/12/04/three-tv-rain-employees-to-leave-network-over-firing-of-host-alexey-korostelev.

57 **"threat to national security"**: Latvian ruling quoted in *Meduza,* December 6, 2022, https://meduza.io/en/feature/2022/12/06/we-made-a-lot-of-stupid-mistakes.

57 **"All the time":** Peskov's comments in *RIA Novesti,* December 6, 2022, https://ria.ru/20221206/dozhd-1836623544.html.

57 **"We were acting":** Sindeyeva comments in *Meduza,* December 6, 2022, https://meduza.io/en/feature/2022/12/06/we-made-a-lot-of-stupid-mistakes.

120   57   **"left Russia to continue":** Krichevskaya's comments in the *New York Times*, December 6, 2022, https://www.nytimes.com/2022/12 /06/world/europe/ukraine-russia -war-latvia-tv-rain-journalism .html.

59   **"story of Germany's descent":** in TV Rain newsroom email to author, December 29, 2022.

60   **"a new episode":** in TV Rain newsroom email to author, January 10, 2023.

60   **ninety-five sources:** See report, "A Guide to Russian Media in the Times of Total Censorship," August 15, 2022, https://www .proekt.media/en/guide-en/russian -media-after-war-en/.

60   **increased from 2.5 million:** In "A Guide to Russian Media in the Times of Total Censorship."

60   **to 1.3 million:** In "A Guide to Russian Media in the Times of Total Censorship."

61   **"battle between democracy":** Biden speech, March 26, 2022, Warsaw, https://www.whitehouse .gov/briefing-room/speeches -remarks/2022/03/26/remarks-by -president-biden-on-the-united -efforts-of-the-free-world-to -support-the-people-of-ukraine/.

63   **survey by the well-respected Levada Center:** For these numbers,

see Levada release, https://www .levada.ru/en/2022/12/12/conflict -with-ukraine-november-2022/.

63   **closed Kremlin-commissioned:** See *Meduza*, November 30, 2022, https:// meduza.io/feature/2022/11/30 /za-peregovory-s-ukrainoy -vystupayut-55-rossiyan-za -prodolzhenie-voyny-tolko-25.

63   **81 percent expressed approval:** See Levada release, https://www.levada.ru/en/2022 /12/12/approval-of-institutions -ratings-of-parties-and -politicians-4/.

CHAPTER FOUR: WARRIORS IN EXILE

65   **"born in 1976":** Many biographical details on Kokorich are taken from his sworn 2018 statement in support of his application for political asylum in the US, the document shared with the author. He later withdrew the application.

67   **"Large countries are behind":** Kokorich article reprinted here: https://www.4freerussia.org /all-power-to-the-bears/.

67   **range of 22,000 kilometers:** From fact sheet of Kokorich's company, Destinus, sent by Kokorich to the author. Information on Destinus on company website at https:// destinus.ch/.

71   **"Conformism of this kind":**
Quote from Russian pollster in
https://cepa.org/article/why
-russians-swallow-propaganda/.

72   **base in the Ryazan region:**
See CNN article, December 6,
2022, https://www.cnn.com/2022
/12/05/europe/ukraine-drone
-russia-air-base-attacks-intl
/index.html.

73   **"A real Russian man":** Quoted
in report on Free Russia Legion in
the *New York Times,* February 12,
2023, https://www.nytimes.com
/2023/02/12/world/europe/russian
-legion-ukraine-war.html.

73   **"terrorist organization":**
Statement of Prosecutor General's
Office at https://epp.genproc.gov
.ru/web/gprf/mass-media/news
?item=85102706.

73   **"There was a large number":**
Quoted in the *New York Times* Free
Russia Legion article, February 12,
2023, https://www.nytimes.com
/2023/02/12/world/europe/russian
-legion-ukraine-war.html.

74   **bitcoin wallet:** See website of
Combat Organization of Anarcho-
Communists at https://boakeng
.noblogs.org/.

74   **"claims responsibility":** Blog
post, July, 2022 at https://boakeng
.noblogs.org/post/2022/07/04
/sabotage-action-on-the-railway
-of-military-unit-55443-vd

-barsovo-51th-arsenal-of-the
-main-rocket-artillery-department
-of-russian-defense-ministry/.

75   **"unscrewing dozens of nuts":**
Vice piece, August 31, 2022, at
https://www.vice.com/en/article
/5d3den/russian-anarchists-are
-sabotaging-railways-to-stop
-putins-war-on-ukraine.

75   **"people waking up":**
BOAK Telegram channel post,
February 25, 2022, in https://
crimethinc.com/2022/02/26
/russian-anarchists-on-resisting
-the-invasion-of-ukraine-updates
-and-analysis#:~:text=The%20
Anarchist%20Black%20Cross%20
of,on%20the%20territory%20
of%20Ukraine.

75   **custom-built armored car:**
See *Radio Free Europe/Radio Free
Liberty* article, February 14, 2023,
https://www.rferl.org/a/russia
-putin-special-train-travel-secret
-ukraine-war/32270737.html.

76   **"passion for destruction":**
Bakunin quote in https://www
.britannica.com/biography
/Mikhail-Bakunin.

76   **"not been given":** In Nikolai
Berdyaev, *The Russian Idea* (The
Centenary Press, 1947), p. 2.

77   **"It was not the Russians":**
Anti-War Committee manifesto at
https://antiwarcommittee.info/en
/committee/.

122   CHAPTER FIVE:
       THE SPIRITUAL RESISTANCE

81   **"then christened":** Quote from Putin's message, December 5, 2014, on Crimea, see https://orthochristian.com/75734.html.

81   **melted-down weapons:** Description of cathedral in *The Conversation,* March 2, 2022, https://theconversation.com/holy-wars-how-a-cathedral-of-guns-and-glory-symbolizes-putins-russia-176786.

82   **"must wake up":** Kirill remarks at cathedral, April 3, 2022, in http://www.patriarchia.ru/db/text/5914188.html?fbclid=IwAR37VW4l-JKWsxj16MhepsDlU2KokIRX__18KQNoA9IJRoJ78Ja8PjlkFP8.

84   **"for a new generation":** Quoted in Yves Hamant, *Alexander Men* (Oakwood Publications, 1995), p. 128.

85   **"For those Christians":** Men's lecture quote in Yves Hamant, *Alexander Men*, p. 138.

85   **from an axe:** Men's murder recounted in Yves Hamant, *Alexander Men*, pp. 3–5.

86   **"sincere atheist":** Yeltsin quote in the *Baltimore Sun,* June 15, 1992, https://www.baltimoresun.com/news/bs-xpm-1992-06-15-1992167118-story.html,

87   **I met in Moscow:** Meeting recounted in author's article in *The Atlantic,* "The Accidental Autocrat," March 2005 issue, https://www.theatlantic.com/magazine/archive/2005/03/the-accidental-autocrat/303725/.

87   **"Power has to be based":** Seminarian quoted in author's piece in *The New Republic,* "The Putin Generation," April 10, 2012, https://newrepublic.com/article/102777/vladimir-putin-russia-protest-maxim-katz-moscow.

88   **top name:** Open letter and list of signatories at https://www.pravmir.com/open-letter-from-priests-in-defence-of-prisoners-in-the-moscow-case/.

88   **"devoid of justice":** Batov quote in the *Moscow Times,* September 19, 2019, https://www.themoscowtimes.com/2019/09/19/russian-priest-who-signed-open-letter-in-support-of-protesters-says-government-threats-not-the-answer-a67345.

88   **"immediate ceasefire":** Open letter reported in *Radio Free Europe/Radio Liberty* article, March 1, 2022, https://www.rferl.org/a/russia-orthodox-clerics-stop-war-ukrane/31730667.html.

90   **"Why Have You Forgotten":** Chapnin's Open Letter in *Public Orthodoxy,* Febuary 6, 2023, https://publicorthodoxy.org/2023/02/06/open-letter-russian-bishops/.

92   **"anti-Soviet agitation":** Cited in his bio details, https://

www.waterstones.com/events/an -evening-with-oleg-radzinsky -all-things-considered/london -piccadilly-the-russian-bookshop.

92   **fewer than 10 percent:** Data in Pew Research Center survey, "Russians Return to Religion, but Not to Church," February 10, 2014, https://www.pewresearch.org /religion/2014/02/10/russians -return-to-religion-but-not-to -church/.

92   **75 percent of Russians:** Data in Pew Research Center survey, "Eastern and Western Europeans Differ on Importance of Religion . . . ," October 29, 2018, https://www.pewresearch.org /religion/2018/10/29/eastern-and -western-europeans-differ-on -importance-of-religion-views -of-minorities-and-key-social -issues/.

92   **47 percent of Russians:** Data in *Russia.Post,* January 18, 2023, https://russiapost.info/society /state_ideology.

CHAPTER SIX:
WAITING FOR NAVALNY

94   **"to those who fight":** On Train Foundation award, see https://www.civilcourageprize .org/. Author attended event on October 24, 2022, at NYU's Kimmel Center.

96   **expressly backed:** Navalny 2011 video on deportations at

YouTube, https://www.youtube .com/watch?v=ICoc2VmGdfw &ab_channel=AlexeyNavalny.

96   **pistol in hand:** Navalny 2007 gun rights video at YouTube, https://www.youtube.com/watch ?v=0VNJiO10SWw&ab_channel =AlexeyNavalny.

97   **"classic example":** Volkov quoted in *Tablet* profile, January 10, 2022, https://www.tabletmag.com /sections/news/articles/leonid -volkov.

98   **"Digital freedoms":** Vokov quoted in bio thumbnail on website of Yale Jackson School of Global Affairs, https:/worldfellows .yale.edu/person/leonid-volkov/.

98   **"integrated moral-ethical system":** Volkov quoted in *Tablet* profile, January 10, 2022, https:// www.tabletmag.com/sections /news/articles/leonid-volkov.

99   **"goal of the Congress":** Kasparov quoted on his website post on the Congress, https://www .kasparov.com/the-congress-of -free-russia-vilnius-august-31 -september-2-2022/.

100   **"I don't know why":** Volkov quoted in the *Globe and Mail,* September 2, 2022, https://www .theglobeandmail.com/world /article-russian-dissidents -squabble-over-how-to-ensure -putins-defeat/.

124   101   **"$200 to pass an exam":**
Pevchikh quote in profile in *The Guardian,* January 22, 2023, https://www.theguardian.com/world/2023/jan/22/navalny-deputy-maria-pevchikh-putin-opposition-corruption-foundation.

101   **"five minutes later":**
Pevchikh *Guardian* profile, January 22, 2023.

101   ***Putin's Palace:*** Video and popularity described in the *Moscow Times,* December 7, 2021, https://www.themoscowtimes.com/2021/12/07/navalnys-putins-palace-investigation-named-most-popular-video-on-russian-youtube-in-2021-a75748.

101   **"It's politics":** Pevchikh *Guardian* profile, January 22, 2023.

101   **"Be scared of nothing":** Cited in Pevchikh *Guardian* profile, January 22, 2023.

104   **shutdown of the Navalny organization in Russia:** A Moscow court labeled Navalny's regional political offices in Russia and the Anti-Corruption Foundation as "extremist" groups; see CNN article, June 9, 2021, https://www.cnn.com/2021/06/09/world/russia-navalny-groups-extremists-intl/index.html.

104   **"Russia's best-known":** See NPR article, December 21, 2013, https://www.npr.org/2013/12/21/255980659/khodorkovsky-a-free-man-in-berlin-after-a-decade-in-russian-prison.

105   **"manual for start-up":** Khodorkovsky talks about his book, see https://khodorkovsky.com/how-to-slay-a-dragon-meduza/. An English translation of the book can be downloaded at https://www.holybooks.com/wp-content/uploads/Mikhail-Khodorkovsky-HOW-DOU-SLAY-A-DRAGON.pdf.

105   **"I know how":** *Blick* article with Khodorkovsky quote posed on Khodorkovsky's website, February 14, 2023, https://khodorkovsky.com/putin-opponent-mikhail-khodorkovsky-is-planning-for-a-change-of-guard-in-the-kremlin/.

106   **"political sponsorship":** Khodorkovsky quote in David E. Hoffman, *The Oligarchs* (PublicAffairs, 2002), p. 101.

107   **"Putin's Culture":** Kasparov op-ed in the *Wall Street Journal,* March 1, 2015, https://www.wsj.com/articles/garry-kasparov-putins-culture-of-fear-and-death-1425249677.

107   **"left-libertarian anarchist":** Ponomarev quoted in *The Guardian,* June 7, 2022, https://www.theguardian.com/world/2022/jun/07/russian-language-ukrainian-tv-channel-aims-to-topple-putin.

107   **"He will not share":**
Ponomarev quoted in *NV* article,
September 2, 2022, https://english
.nv.ua/nation/russian-opposition
-figure-navalny-has-imperialist
-views-50267423.html.

107   **"most powerful":** Ponomarev
quoted in *NV,* September 2, 2022.

108   **"future model for Russia":**
Navalny *Washington Post* op-ed,
September 30, 2022, https://www
.washingtonpost.com/opinions
/2022/09/30/alexei-navalny
-parliamentary-republic-russia
-ukraine/.

108   **scandal surfaced:** Volkov
episode recounted in *Radio Svoboda*
article, March 9, 2023, https://
www.svoboda.org/a/leonid
-volkov-obyavil-o-priostanovke

-publichnoy-deyateljnosti
/32310254.html.

109   **"Volkov made a mistake":**
Navalny's social media remarks in
the *Moscow Times,* March 22, 2023,
https://www.themoscowtimes.com
/2023/03/22/maria-pevchikh-to
-replace-leonid-volkov-as-head
-of-navalny-foundation-board
-a80581.

109   **"The fact is":** Navalny's
remarks to Moscow City Court,
February 20, 2021, posted on
Rights in Russia.org website,
https://www.rightsinrussia.org
/navalny-2/.

111   **"probably" approved:**
Litvinenko finding in BBC News
article, January 21, 2016, https://
www.bbc.com/news/uk-35370819.

Columbia Global Reports is a publishing imprint from Columbia University that commissions authors to produce works of original thinking and on-site reporting from all over the world, on a wide range of topics. Our books are short—novella-length, and readable in a few hours—but ambitious. They offer new ways of looking at and understanding the major issues of our time. Most readers are curious and busy. Our books are for them.

Subscribe to our newsletter, and learn more about Columbia Global Reports at globalreports.columbia.edu.